Vagabonding

Vagabonding

AN UNCOMMON GUIDE

TO THE ART

OF LONG-TERM

WORLD TRAVEL

Rolf Potts

VILLARD **V** NEW YORK

Published in the United States by Villard
Books, an imprint of The Random House
Publishing Group, a division of Random
House, Inc., New York, and simultaneously in
Canada by Random House of Canada Lim-
ited, Toronto.

VILLARD and "V" CIRCLED Design are registered
trademarks of Random House, Inc.

Grateful acknowledgment is made to the following for permission to reprint previously
published material:
Outside magazine: Excerpts from "Exotic
Places Made Me Do It" by Tim Cahill (*Outside,* March 2002). Copyright © 2002 by
Mariah Publications Corporation. Reprinted
by permission of *Outside* magazine.
Random House, Inc.: Excerpts from *Vagabonding in Europe and North Africa* by Ed
Buryn. Copyright © 1971 by Ed Buryn. Used
by permission of Random House, Inc.

Library of Congress Cataloging-in-Publication
Data
Potts, Rolf.
Vagabonding: an uncommon guide to the art
of long-term world travel/Rolf Potts.
p. cm.
ISBN 978-0-8129-9218-2
1. Travel. 2. Sabbatical leave. I. Title.
G151.P69 2003   910—dc21
2002069029
www.villard.com
Vagabonding website: www.vagabonding.net

Printed in the United States of America
19 18 17 16 15 14 13 12 11 10

Book design by Judith Stagnitto Abbate

For two teachers:

GEORGE D. POTTS,
prairie naturalist and
dreamer extraordinaire

And in memory of

JOHN FREDIN,
mentor and friend
(1930–2000)

You air that serves me breath to speak!
You objects that call from diffusion my meanings
   and give them shape!
You that wraps me and all things in delicate equible
   showers!
You paths worn in irregular hollows by the road-
   sides!
   I believe you are latent with unseen existences,
      you are so dear to me.

**—WALT WHITMAN, "SONG OF
THE OPEN ROAD"**

Vagabonding—n.   (1) The act of leaving behind the orderly world to travel independently for an extended period of time.   (2) A privately meaningful manner of travel that emphasizes creativity, adventure, awareness, simplicity, discovery, independence, realism, self-reliance, and the growth of the spirit.   (3) A deliberate way of living that makes freedom to travel possible.

Preface

HOW TO USE THIS BOOK

Many travel books can help prepare you for an overseas trip, but this book—in sharing a simple and time-honored ethic—can teach you how to travel for the rest of your life. Some books, in offering encyclopedic (and often redundant) travel information, create the illusion that the best way to plan for an extended trip is to micromanage it. This book, in offering you only the advice you need to prepare for (and adapt to) the road, encourages you to enrich your travels with the vivid joys of uncertainty. And while some travel books become obsolete after one reading, this book will shed new perspectives and resonate in new ways as your travel career progresses.

This book views long-term travel not as an escape but as an adventure and a passion—a way of overcoming your fears and living life to the fullest. In reading it, you will find out how to gain an impressive wealth (of travel time) through simplicity. You will find out how to discover and deal with new experiences and adventures on the road. And, as much as anything, you will find out how to travel the world on your own terms, by overcoming the myths and pretentions that threaten to cheapen your experience.

If you've ever felt the urge to travel for extended periods of time but aren't sure how to find the time and freedom to do it, this is the book for you. If you've traveled before but felt something vital was missing from the experience, this book is for you, too.

This book is not for daredevils and thrill seekers but for anyone willing to make an uncommon choice that allows you to travel the world for weeks and months at a time, improvising (and saving money) as you go.

If this sounds like an intriguing possibility, then by all means read on. . . .

Contents

All I mark as my own you shall offset it with your
    own,
Else it were time lost listening to me.

—WALT WHITMAN, "SONG OF MYSELF"

How to Win and Influence Yourself

Not so long ago, as I was taking a slow, decrepit old mail steamer down Burma's Irrawaddy River, I ran out of things to read. When the riverboat called at a small town called Pyay, I dashed ashore and bought the only English-language book I could find for sale: a beat-up copy of Dale Carnegie's *How to Win Friends and*

Influence People, which I proceeded to read as we slowly steamed toward Rangoon.

Somehow, I'd gone through my entire life without ever having read a self-help book. Carnegie's advice, as it turned out, was a charming mix of common sense ("be a good listener"), good advice ("show respect for the other man's opinions"), and antique notions ("don't forget how profoundly women are interested in clothes"). Having enjoyed the book on the river, I gave it away in Rangoon and temporarily forgot about it.

About a month later, I was approached to write a book about the art and attitude of long-term travel. Since I'd primarily been endorsing this vagabonding ethic through the narrative stories I'd written for *Salon.com,* I figured I should probably do some research into the structure and format of advice books. Thus, in the process of trying to relocate a copy of *How to Win Friends and Influence People,* I discovered that the advice and self-help book market has changed a lot since Carnegie's day. Nearly every human activity, desire, and demographic, it seems, is now catered to by some kind of inspirational book. The *Chicken Soup for the Soul* and *Don't Sweat the Small Stuff* series by themselves nearly required their own section of the bookstore.

Standing there amid the shelves—and bewildered at the variety—I began to imagine a vagabonding publishing empire: not just *Vagabonding,* but *Vagabonding for Teens. Vagabonding for Singles. Vagabonding for Golfers. Vagabonding Your Wardrobe. The Ten-Week Vagabonding Diet. A Vagabonding Christmas. A Baby's First Vagabonding. 101 Zesty Vagabonding Recipes. All I Ever Really Needed to Know I Learned While Vagabonding.* And so on.

In the end, I left the bookstore without picking up a single book. I decided that I would write the book the only way I knew how: from experience, from passion, and from common sense.

If at times this book seems unorthodox, well, good. Vagabonding itself is unorthodox.

As for the word *vagabonding,* I used to think it was my own invention. This was back in 1998, when I was first pitching an adventure travel column to *Salon.com.* At the time, I wanted a succinct word to describe what I was doing: leaving the ordered world to travel on the cheap for an extended period of time. *Backpacking* seemed too vague a description, *globe-trotting* sounded too pretentious, and *touring* rang a bit lame. Consequently, I put a playful spin on the word *vagabond*—the old, Latin-derived term that refers to a wanderer with no fixed home—and came up with *vagabonding.*

I'd almost convinced myself that I'd given hip new phrasing to a certain attitude of travel when I discovered a dog-eared paperback entitled *Vagabonding in Europe and North Africa* on the shelf of a used bookstore in Tel Aviv. Written by an American named Ed Buryn, the book had not only been published before my travel column hit the Internet but had been written before I was born. And in spite of its occasional hippie-era phrasing ("avoid your travel agent like he was the cops and go out to find out about the world by yourself"), I found *Vagabonding in Europe and North Africa* to be a fine collection of advice, a levelheaded and insightful pre–Lonely Planet take on the nuts, bolts, and philosophy of independent travel. Consequently, discovering Ed Buryn's book was not discouraging so much as it was liberating: It made me realize that, whatever name you give it, the act of vagabonding is not an isolated trend so much as it is (to crib a Greil Marcus phrase) a "spectral connection between people long separated by place and time, but somehow speaking the same language."

I have since seen reference to the word *vagabonding* as early as 1871 (in Mark Twain's *Roughing It*), but I've never found it in any dictionary. In a way, it's a kind of nonsense word—playfully adapted to describe a travel phenomenon that was already out there when Walt Whitman wrote, "I or you pocketless of a dime may purchase the pick of the earth."

Thus, a part of me wants to keep the notion of vagabonding partly rooted in nonsense: as indeterminate, slightly slippery, and open to interpretation as the travel experience itself.

So, as you prepare to read the book, just keep in mind what martial arts master Bruce Lee said: "Research your own experiences for the truth. . . . Absorb what is useful. . . . Add what is specifically your own. . . . The creating individual is more than any style or system."

On the road, the same holds true for vagabonding.

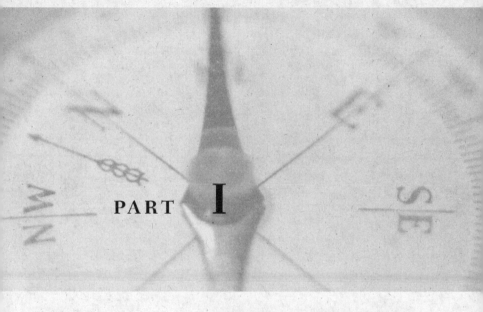

PART I

Vagabonding

CHAPTER 1

From this hour I ordain myself loos'd of limits and
   imaginary lines,
Going where I list, my own master total and absolute,
Listening to others, considering well what they say,
Pausing, searching, receiving, contemplating,
Gently, but with undeniable will divesting myself of
   the holds that would hold me.

—WALT WHITMAN, "SONG OF
THE OPEN ROAD"

Declare Your Independence

Of all the outrageous throwaway lines one hears in movies, there is one that stands out for me. It doesn't come from a madcap comedy, an esoteric science-fiction flick, or a special-effects-laden action thriller. It comes from Oliver Stone's *Wall Street,* when the Charlie Sheen character—a promising big shot in the stock market—is telling his girlfriend about his dreams.

"I think if I can make a bundle of cash before I'm thirty and get out of this racket," he says, "I'll be able to ride my motorcycle across China."

When I first saw this scene on video a few years ago, I nearly fell out of my seat in astonishment. After all, Charlie Sheen or anyone else could work for eight months as a *toilet cleaner* and have enough money to ride a motorcycle across China. Even if they didn't yet have their own motorcycle, another couple months of scrubbing toilets would earn them enough to buy one when they got to China.

The thing is, most Americans probably wouldn't find this movie scene odd. For some reason, we see long-term travel to faraway lands as a recurring dream or an exotic temptation, but not something that applies to the here and now. Instead—out of our insane duty to fear, fashion, and monthly payments on things we don't really need—we quarantine our travels to short, frenzied bursts. In this way, as we throw our wealth at an abstract notion called "lifestyle," travel becomes just another accessory—a smooth-edged, encapsulated experience that we purchase the same way we buy clothing and furniture.

Not long ago, I read that nearly a quarter of a million short-term monastery- and convent-based vacations had been booked and sold by tour agents in the year 2000. Spiritual enclaves from Greece to Tibet were turning into hot tourist draws, and travel pundits attributed this "solace boom" to the fact that "busy overachievers are seeking a simpler life."

What nobody bothered to point out, of course, is that purchasing a package vacation to find a simpler life is kind of like using a mirror to see what you look like when you aren't looking into the mirror. All that is really sold is the romantic *notion* of a simpler life, and—just as no amount of turning your head or flicking your eyes will allow you to unselfconsciously see yourself in the looking glass—no combination of one-week or ten-day vacations will truly take you away from the life you lead at home.

Ultimately, this shotgun wedding of time and money has a way of keeping us in a holding pattern. The more we associate experience with cash value, the more we think that money is what we need to live. And the more we associate money with life, the more we convince ourselves that we're too poor to buy our freedom. With this kind of mind-set, it's no wonder so many Americans think extended overseas travel is the exclusive realm of students, counterculture dropouts, and the idle rich.

In reality, long-term travel has nothing to do with demographics—age, ideology, income—and everything to do with personal outlook. Long-term travel isn't about being a college student; it's about being a student of daily life. Long-term travel isn't an act of rebellion against society; it's an act of common sense within society. Long-term travel doesn't require a massive "bundle of cash"; it requires only that we walk through the world in a more deliberate way.

This deliberate way of walking through the world has always been intrinsic to the time-honored, quietly available travel tradition known as "vagabonding."

Vagabonding involves taking an extended time-out from your normal life—six weeks, four months, two years—to travel the world on your own terms.

But beyond travel, vagabonding is an outlook on life. Vagabonding is about using the prosperity and possibility of the information age to increase your personal options instead of your personal possessions. Vagabonding is about looking for adventure in normal life, and normal life within adventure. Vagabonding is an attitude—a friendly interest in people, places, and things that makes a person an explorer in the truest, most vivid sense of the word.

Vagabonding is not a lifestyle, nor is it a trend. It's just an uncommon way of looking at life—a value adjustment from which action naturally follows. And, as much as anything, vagabonding is about time—our only real commodity—and how we choose to use it.

Sierra Club founder John Muir (an ur-vagabonder if there ever was one) used to express amazement at the well-heeled travelers who would visit Yosemite only to rush away after a few hours of sightseeing. Muir called these folks the "time-poor"—people who were so obsessed with tending their material wealth and social standing that they couldn't spare the time to truly experience the splendor of California's Sierra wilderness. One of Muir's Yosemite visitors in the summer of 1871 was Ralph Waldo Emerson, who gushed upon seeing the sequoias, "It's a wonder that we can see these trees and not wonder more." When Emerson scurried off a couple hours later, however, Muir speculated wryly about whether the famous transcendentalist had really seen the trees in the first place.

Nearly a century later, naturalist Edwin Way Teale used Muir's example to lament the frenetic pace of modern society. "Freedom as John Muir knew it," he wrote in his 1956 book *Autumn Across America*, "with its wealth of time, its unregimented days, its latitude of choice . . . such freedom seems more rare, more difficult to attain, more remote with each new generation."

But Teale's lament for the deterioration of personal freedom was just as hollow a generalization in 1956 as it is now. As John Muir was well aware, vagabonding has never been regulated by the fickle public definition of lifestyle. Rather, it has always been a private choice within a society that is constantly urging us to do otherwise.

This is a book about living that choice.

PART **II**

Getting Started

If you have built castles in the air, your work need not be lost; that is where they should be. Now put the foundations under them.

—HENRY DAVID THOREAU, *WALDEN*.

Earn Your Freedom

There's a story that comes from the tradition of the Desert Fathers, an order of Christian monks who lived in the wastelands of Egypt about seventeen hundred years ago. In the tale, a couple of monks named Theodore and Lucius shared the acute desire to go out and see the world. Since they'd made vows of contemplation, however, this was not something they were allowed to do. So, to satiate their wanderlust, Theodore and Lucius learned to "mock their temptations" by relegating their travels to the future. When the summertime came, they said to each other, "We will leave in the winter." When the winter came, they said, "We will leave in the summer." They went on like this for over fifty years, never once leaving the monastery or breaking their vows.

Most of us, of course, have never taken such vows—but we choose to live like monks anyway, rooting ourselves to a home or a career and using the future as a kind of phony ritual that justifies the present. In this way, we end up spending (as Thoreau put it) "the best part of one's life earning money in order to enjoy a questionable liberty during the least valuable part of it." We'd love to drop all and explore the world outside, we tell ourselves, but the time never seems right. Thus, given an unlimited amount of choices, we make none. Settling into our lives, we get so obsessed with holding on to our domestic certainties that we forget why we desired them in the first place.

Vagabonding is about gaining the courage to loosen your grip on the so-called certainties of this world. Vagabonding is about refusing to exile travel to some other, seemingly more appropriate, time of your life. Vagabonding is about taking control of your circumstances instead of passively waiting for them to decide your fate.

Thus, the question of how and when to start vagabonding is not really a question at all. Vagabonding starts now. Even if the practical reality of travel is still months or years away, vagabonding begins the moment you stop making excuses, start saving money, and begin to look at maps with the narcotic tingle of possibility. From here, the reality of vagabonding comes into sharper focus as you adjust your worldview and begin to embrace the exhilarating uncertainty that true travel promises.

In this way, vagabonding is not a merely a ritual of getting immunizations and packing suitcases. Rather, it's the ongoing practice of looking and learning, of facing fears and altering habits, of cultivating a new fascination with people and places. This attitude is not something you can pick up at the airport counter with your boarding pass; it's a process that starts at home. It's a process by which you first test the waters that will pull you to wonderful new places.

> If one advances confidently in the direction of his dreams, and endeavors to live the life which he has imagined, he will meet with a success unexpected in common hours. He will put some things behind, will pass an invisible boundary; new, universal, and more liberal laws will begin to establish themselves around and within him.
>
> —HENRY DAVID THOREAU, *WALDEN*

During this process, you may even find that you aren't up for the uncertainties and adaptations that vagabonding requires. "Vagabonding," as Ed Buryn bluntly put it thirty years ago, "is not for comfort hounds, sophomoric misanthropes or poolside faint-hearts, whose thin convictions won't stand up to the problems that come along." In saying this, Buryn wasn't being a snob. After all, vagabonding involves sacrifices, and its particular sacrifices are not for everyone.

Thus, it's important to keep in mind that you should never go vagabonding out of a vague sense of fashion or obligation. Vagabonding is not a social gesture, nor is it a moral high ground. It's not a seamless twelve-step program of travel correctness or a political statement that demands the reinvention of society. Rather, it's a personal act that demands only the realignment of self.

If this personal realignment is not something you're

willing to confront (or, of course, if world travel isn't your idea of a good time), you have the perfect right to leave vagabonding to those who feel the calling.

Ironically, the best litmus test for measuring your vagabonding gumption is found not in travel but in the process of earning your freedom to travel. Earning your freedom, of course, involves work—and work is intrinsic to vagabonding for psychic reasons as much as financial ones.

To see the psychic importance of work, one need look no further than people who travel the world on family money. Sometimes referred to as "trustafarians," these folks are among the most visible and least happy wanderers in the travel milieu. Draping themselves in local fashions, they flit from one exotic travel scene to another, compulsively volunteering in local political causes, experimenting with exotic intoxicants, and dabbling in every non-Western religion imaginable. Talk to them, and they'll tell you they're searching for something "meaningful."

> And they say in truth that a man is made of desire. As his desire is, so is his faith. As his faith is, so are his works. As his works are, so he becomes.
>
> —THE SUPREME TEACHING OF THE UPANISHADS

What they're really looking for, however, is the reason why they started traveling in the first place. Because they never worked for their freedom, their travel experiences have no personal reference—no connection to the rest of their lives. They are spending plenty of time and money on the road, but they never spent enough of themselves to begin with. Thus, their experience of travel has a diminished sense of value.

Thoreau touched on this same notion in *Walden*. "Which would have advanced the most at the end of a month," he posited, "the boy who had made his own jackknife from the ore which he had dug and smelted, reading as much as would be necessary for this—or the boy who had . . . received a Rodgers' penknife from his father? Which would be most likely to cut his fingers?"

At a certain level, the idea that freedom is tied to labor might seem a bit depressing. It shouldn't be. For all the amazing experiences that await you in distant lands, the "meaningful" part of travel always starts at home, with a personal investment in the wonders to come.

"I don't like work," says Marlow in Joseph Conrad's *Heart of Darkness*, "but I like what is in the work—the chance to find yourself." Marlow wasn't referring to vagabonding, but the notion still applies. Work is not just an activity that generates funds and creates desire; it's the vagabonding gestation period, wherein you earn your integrity, start making plans, and get your proverbial act together. Work is a time to dream about travel and write notes to yourself, but it's also the time to tie up your loose ends. Work is when you confront the problems you might otherwise be tempted to run away from. Work is how you

> Wanting to travel reflects a positive attitude. You want to see, to grow in experience, and presumably to become more whole as a human being. Vagabonding takes this a step further: It promotes the chances of sustaining and strengthening this positive attitude. As a vagabond, you begin to face your fears now and then instead of continuously sidestepping them in the name of convenience. You build an attitude that makes life more rewarding, which in turn makes it easier to keep doing it. It's called positive feedback, and it works.
>
> —ED BURYN, *VAGABONDING IN EUROPE AND NORTH AFRICA*

settle your financial *and* emotional debts—so that your travels are not an escape from your real life but a *discovery* of your real life.

On a practical level, there are countless ways to earn your travels. On the road, I have met vagabonders of all ages, from all backgrounds and walks of life. I've met secretaries, bankers, and policemen who've quit their jobs and are taking a peripatetic pause before starting something new. I've met lawyers, stockbrokers, and social workers who have negotiated months off as they take their careers to new locations. I've met talented specialists—waiters, Web designers, strippers—who find they can fund months of travel on a few weeks of work. I've met musicians, truck drivers, and employment counselors who are taking extended time off between gigs. I've met semiretired soldiers and engineers and businessmen who've reserved a year or two for travel before dabbling in something else. Some of the most prolific vagabonders I've met are seasonal workers—carpenters, park service workers, commercial fishermen—who winter every year in warm and exotic parts of the world. Other folks—teachers, doctors, bartenders, journalists—have opted to take their very careers on the road, alternating work and travel as they see fit.

Many vagabonders don't even maintain a steady job description, taking short-term work only as it serves to fund their travels and their passions. In *Generation X,* Douglas Coupland defined this kind of work as an "anti-sabbatical"—a job approached "with the sole intention of staying for a limited period of time (often one year) . . . to raise enough funds to partake in another, more personally meaningful activity." Before I got into writing, a whole slew of antisabbaticals (landscaping, retail sales, temp work) earned me my vagabonding time.

Of all the antisabbaticals that funded my travels, however, no experience was quite as vivid as the two years I spent teaching English in Pusan, South Korea. In addition to learning tons about Asian social customs through my work, I discovered that the simple act of *walking to work* was itself an exercise in possibility. On a given day in Korea, I was equally likely to be greeted by a Buddhist monk wearing Air Jordans as I was by a woman in a stewardess uniform handing out promotional toilet tissue. I eventually stopped noticing such details as children screaming "hello," old men urinating in public, and vegetable-truck loudspeakers blasting "Edelweiss." After two years on the job, I actually found myself fighting boredom as I crooned "California Dreaming" with my salaryman tutees and a roomful of miniskirted seventeen-year-old karaoke "hostesses." And on top of all this, the pay was pretty good.

> We need the possibility of escape as surely as we need hope; without it the life of the cities would drive all men into crime or drugs or psychoanalysis.
>
> —EDWARD ABBEY, *DESERT SOLITAIRE*

However you choose to fund your travel freedom, keep in mind that your work is an active part of your travel attitude. Even if your antisabbatical job isn't your life's calling, approach your work with a spirit of faith, mindfulness, and thrift. In such a manner, Thoreau was able to meet all his living expenses at Walden Pond by working just six weeks a year. Since vagabonding is more involved than freelance philosophizing, however, you might have to invest a bit more time in scraping together your travel funds.

Regardless of how long it takes to earn your freedom, remember that you are laboring for more than just a vacation.

A vacation, after all, merely rewards work. Vagabonding justifies it.

Ultimately, then, the first step of vagabonding is simply a matter of making work serve your interests, instead of the other way around. Believe it or not, this is a radical departure from how most people view work and leisure.

A few years ago, *Escape* magazine editor Joe Robinson spearheaded a petition campaign called Work to Live. The goal of this movement was to pass a law that would increase American vacation time to three weeks after one year on the job, and to four weeks after three years. The rationale was that Americans place too much emphasis on work—that all we have to look forward to from day to day is a long tunnel of eleven and a half months of work every year. "The leading casualty of all this is our time," said Robinson, "that commodity we seemed to have so much of back in sixth grade, when the clock on the wall never seemed to move."

Robinson's campaign was a worthy one, and it found plenty of support at the grassroots level (and a fair amount of antagonism in corporate circles). Amid all this publicity, however, I was amazed that nobody was subversive enough to point out the obvious: As citizens of a stable, prosperous democracy, any one of us has the power to create our *own* free time, outside the whims of federal laws and private-sector policies. Indeed, if the clock appears to move faster than it did in sixth grade, it's only because we haven't actualized our power as adults to set our own recess schedule.

To actualize this power, we merely need to make

strategic use (if only for a few weeks or months) of a time-honored personal-freedom technique, popularly known as "quitting." And, despite its pejorative implication, quitting need not be as reckless as it sounds. Many people are able to create vagabonding time through "constructive quitting"—that is, negotiating with their employers for special sabbaticals and long-term leaves of absence.

Even leaving your job in a more permanent manner need not be a negative act—especially in an age when work is likely to be defined by job specialization and the fragmentation of tasks. Whereas working a job with the intention of quitting it might have been an act of recklessness a hundred years ago, it is more and more often becoming an act of common sense in an age of portable skills and diversified employment options. Keeping this in mind, don't worry that your extended travels might leave you with a "gap" on your résumé. Rather, you should enthusiastically and unapologetically *include your vagabonding experience on your résumé* when you return. List the job skills travel has taught you: independence, flexibility, negotiation, planning, boldness, self-sufficiency, improvisation. Speak frankly and confidently about your travel experiences—the odds are, your next employer will be interested and impressed (and a wee bit envious).

> A lot of us first aspired to far-ranging travel and exotic adventure early in our teens; these ambitions are, in fact, adolescent in nature, which I find an inspiring idea. . . . Thus, when we allow ourselves to imagine as we once did, we know, with a sudden jarring clarity, that if we don't go right now, we're never going to do it. And we'll be haunted by our unrealized dreams and know that we have sinned against ourselves gravely.
>
> —TIM CAHILL, "EXOTIC PLACES MADE ME DO IT"

As Pico Iyer pointed out, the act of quitting "means not giving up, but moving on; changing direction not because something doesn't agree with you, but because you don't agree with something. It's not a complaint, in other words, but a positive choice, and not a stop in one's journey, but a step in a better direction. Quitting—whether a job or a habit—means taking a turn so as to be sure you're still moving in the direction of your dreams."

In this way, quitting a job to go vagabonding should never be seen as the end of something grudging and unpleasant. Rather, it's a vital step in *beginning* something new and wonderful.

> And so I stand among you as one that offers a small message of hope, that first, there are always people who dare to seek on the margin of society, who are not dependent on social acceptance, not dependent on social routine, and prefer a kind of free-floating existence.
>
> —THOMAS MERTON, *THE ASIAN JOURNAL OF THOMAS MERTON*

Tip Sheet

SABBATICALS, UNPAID LEAVE, AND QUITTING YOUR JOB

Six Months Off: How to Plan, Negotiate, and Take the Break You Need Without Burning Bridges or Going Broke, by Hope Dlugozima, James Scott, and David Sharp (Henry Holt, 1996)
A detailed, action-oriented how-to book about planning and negotiating employee sabbaticals and leaves of absence.

Time Off from Work: Using Sabbaticals to Enhance Your Life While Keeping Your Career on Track, by Lisa Angowski Rogak (John Wiley & Sons, 1994)
A practical guide to planning and implementing sabbaticals. Includes tips on long-term financial planning.

I-Resign.com (http://www.i-resign.com)
Online advice on how to diplomatically quit your job, sample resignation letters, discussion boards about quitting, tips on finding a new job.

FINDING JOBS AND CAREERS OVERSEAS

A fantastic way to earn travel money is to find work overseas. Such work will not only fund your travels but will also teach you intuitive lessons about how to act and react in foreign cultures. Highly recommended as a way to enable and inspire your vagabonding career.

Work Worldwide: International Career Strategies for the Adventurous Job Seeker, by Nancy Mueller (Avalon Travel Publishing, 2000)
Step-by-step advice on how to research, apply for, and get an international job.

Work Abroad: The Complete Guide to Finding a Job Overseas, by Clayton A. Hubbs, Susan Griffith, and William T. Nolting (Transitions Abroad, 2000)
A practical guide for finding jobs overseas. Includes country-by-country listings of employers and organizations.

Overseas Jobs (http://www.overseasjobs.com/)
Online information and resources regarding international

jobs, careers, and work. Country-specific online job list-ings.

Overseas Digest (http://overseasdigest.com/)
Employment tips and cross-cultural information for Ameri-cans working abroad.

Teaching English Overseas: A Job Guide for Americans and Canadians, by Jeff Mohamed (English International, 2000)
A comprehensive practical guide for finding jobs teaching English overseas. Includes detailed information and ad-vice on choosing a training program, teaching without training, and how to conduct a successful job search. Useful companion website at http://www.english-inter national.com/.

Dave's ESL Café (http://eslcafe.com/)
One of the oldest and most useful Internet resources for overseas English teachers and job seekers. Includes dis-cussion forums and job listings.

INTERNATIONAL EMPLOYMENT REFERENCES

International Jobs: Where They Are, How to Get Them, by Eric Kocher and Nina Segal (Perseus Press, 1999)

International Jobs Directory: A Guide to Over 1001 Em-ployers, by Ronald L. Krannich and Caryl Rae Krannich (Impact Publications, 1999)

The Directory of Jobs and Careers Abroad, by Elisabeth Roberts and Jonathan Packer (Vacation-Work, 2000)

One of the big issues these days among potential vagabonders is whether or not it's safe to travel overseas anymore.

The short answer to this concern is that *traveling around the world is statistically no more dangerous than traveling across your hometown.* Indeed, as with home, most dangers and annoyances on the road revolve around sickness, theft, and accidents (see chapter 7)—not political violence or terrorism.

Should political violence or terrorism capture headlines, however, the secret to avoiding it is not to cancel your travel plans but to simply keep yourself informed. Just because the evening news shows unrest in a southern Lebanon refugee camp, for instance, doesn't necessarily mean it's dangerous to visit Beirut or Galilee (or, for that matter, other parts of southern Lebanon). By the same token, the evening news might habitually ignore the political situation in West Africa, but that doesn't mean it's safe to visit Sierra Leone or Liberia. Obviously, then, planning and monitoring your destinations will require that you look past the evening news. Online resources such as U.S. State Department Travel Warnings and World Travel Watch (see below) make good starting points for assessing the current safety situation in any given part of the world.

Even if you accidentally find yourself in a dangerous area as you travel, the key to keeping safe is knowing and talking to the locals (who can tell you where specific dangers lurk), patronizing mom-and-pop businesses (which are never targeted in political attacks), avoiding a loud or flashy appearance (this includes dogmatic debates of religion and politics), and traveling outside of predictable tourist patterns (which are easier to target by troublemakers). In short, the engaged and humble attitude of vagabonding will naturally lend to a safer journey. Should the security situation seem especially tense in a region, go a step further and avoid hangouts that cater exclusively to foreigners (expat bars, Hard Rock Cafes, and the like), stay away from public demonstrations and crowds (this includes small bands of drunks and rabble-rousers), and don't share your travel plans or lodging arrangements with strangers.

On a final note, keep in mind that most people in the world will see you not as a political entity or an appendage of the "Great Satan" but as a guest to their country. Even if they vehemently disagree with your country's policies and practices, they will invariably honor your individuality and regard you with hospitality and respect. You'd never guess this by watching the evening news, of course, but travel allows you to experience the nuances of the world in a way that mass media never will.

U.S. State Department Travel Warnings *State Department Consular Information Sheets (found online at http://travel.state.gov/travel_warnings.html) are available for every country of the world. They describe national entry requirements, currency regulations, unusual health conditions, the crime and security situations, political disturbances, and areas of instability. In the event of a specific and current danger in a country, a special "Travel Warning" is posted alongside the consular information.*

World Travel Watch (http://www.worldtravelwatch.com) *Travel publishers Larry Habegger and James O'Reilly have been writing this weekly travel safety and security update since 1985. It includes succinct, current, and useful information about dangers and disturbances (and odd happenings in general) around the world.*

"A Safe Trip Abroad" Online Tip Sheet *Available online (http://travel.state.gov/asafetripabroad.html), this Department of State tip sheet has good, basic information for keeping out of danger overseas. Included are tips for staying safe from pickpockets and general crime, as well as from political violence and terrorism. Online links lead to specific tip sheets on travel to the Caribbean, Central and South America, China, Mexico, the Middle East, Russia, and South Asia.*

The World's Most Dangerous Places, by Robert Young Pelton (Harper Resource, 2000) *An extensive guide to the danger zones of the world by journalist Robert Pelton. This book evaluates the danger factor in destinations around the globe (including the United States) and provides relevant historical, cultural, and geographical information. "The message is that travel can be dangerous if you want it to be and it can be very safe if you want it to be," writes Pelton. "Even in a war zone."*

For a fully updated and linkable online version of this resource guide, surf to http://vagabonding.net/ and follow the "Resources" link.

VAGABONDING
VOICES

For me, the experience of travel is not only what I'm seeing but also what I have chosen to leave behind, even for a short time, and the perspective I gain from doing that. The hardest thing about travel is deciding to go. Once you've made that commitment, the rest of it is easy. And, despite the anxiety that comes with these issues, my travel experience would not be the same without them. I remember stopping my motorcycle just outside the Bayon complex at Angkor Wat, Cambodia, so I could absorb the scene in front of me. I was overwhelmed with the most awesome feeling of gratitude and pride. I was proud of myself for being there—because I'd worked hard to get there and I knew it. But also for quitting a great job, because I know there is more out there.

—REBECCA MARKEY, 28,
EMPLOYMENT COUNSELOR, ONTARIO

Don't wait around. Don't get old and make excuses. Save a couple thousand dollars. Sell your car. Get a world atlas. Start looking at every page and tell yourself that you *can* go there. You *can* live there. Are there sacrifices to be made? Of course. Is it worth it? Absolutely. The only way you'll find out is to get on the plane and go. And let me tell you something. That first morning, when you are in your country of choice, away from all of the conventions of a typical, everyday lifestyle, looking around at your totally new surroundings, hearing strange languages, smelling strange, new smells, you'll know exactly what I'm talking about. You'll feel like the luckiest person in the world.

—JASON GASPERO, 31,
NEWSLETTER EDITOR, HAWAII

———

There is a very satisfying feeling I get when I work hard and make my own way. It makes me feel like a conqueror, like I've "made it." I lived for most of a year in Europe pretty much hand-to-mouth, which was stressful at times for sure, but it was very challenging and forced me to be creative. This, to me, was a big part of the experience—I learned a lot about myself and my capabilities.

—JOHN BOCSKAY, 30,
TEACHER, NEW YORK

Walt Whitman

Allons! whoever you are, come travel with me!
—WALT WHITMAN, "SONG OF THE OPEN ROAD"

Should vagabonding have a patron saint, it would be the nineteenth-century poet Walt Whitman—if for no reason other than "Song of the Open Road," his infectiously joyous ode to the spirit of travel.

Born in 1819 to a working-class family in New York, Whitman entered the working world as an office boy at age eleven. It was here, and at his later employment as a printer's apprentice, that he developed a passion for self-education—as well as an eye for finding uncommon beauty in the common activity of daily life. Whitman eventually moved on to work as a journalist, but his real life's work was *Leaves of Grass,* a collection of free-spirited verse that grew to more than three hundred poems by the time of his death in 1892.

As a youth, Whitman was particularly inspired by his daily ferry trips from Brooklyn to Manhattan, which instilled in him a lasting appreciation for the uncommon joys and vivid details of travel. And while his later travels took him to budding American outposts such as New Orleans and Denver, it is this celebration of simple movement and possibility that gives "Song of the Open Road" its visceral and inclusive energy:

To see nothing anywhere but what
*   you may reach it and pass it,*
To conceive no time, however
*   distant, but what you may*
*   reach it and pass it,*
To look up or down no road but it
*   stretches and waits for you,*
To know the universe itself as a
*   road, as many roads, as roads*
*   for traveling souls.*

CHAPTER 3

From all your herds, a cup or two of milk,

From all your granaries, a loaf of bread,

In all your palace, only half a bed:

Can man use more? And do you own the rest?

—ANCIENT SANSKRIT POEM

Keep It Simple

In March 1989, the *Exxon Valdez* struck a reef off the coast of Alaska, resulting in the largest oil spill in U.S. history. Initially viewed as an ecological disaster, this catastrophe did wonders to raise environmental awareness among average Americans. As television images of oil-choked sea otters and dying shorebirds were beamed across the country, pop environmentalism grew into a national craze.

Instead of conserving more and consuming less, however, many Americans sought to save the earth by purchasing "environmental" products. Energy-efficient home appliances flew off the shelves, health-food sales boomed, and reusable canvas shopping bags became vogue in strip malls from Jacksonville to Jackson Hole. Credit card companies began to earmark a small percentage of profits for conservation groups, thus encouraging consumers to "help the environment" by striking off on idealistic shopping binges.

Such shopping sprees and health-food purchases did very little to improve the state of the planet, of course—but most people managed to feel a little better about the situation without having to make any serious lifestyle changes.

This notion—that material investment is somehow more important to life than personal investment—is exactly what leads so many of us to believe we could never afford to go vagabonding. The more our life options get paraded around as consumer options, the more we forget that there's a difference between the two. Thus, having convinced ourselves that buying things is the only way to play an active role in the world, we fatalistically conclude that we'll never be rich enough to purchase a long-term travel experience.

Fortunately, the world need not be a consumer product. As with environmental integrity, long-term travel isn't something you buy into; it's something you give to yourself.

Indeed, the freedom to go vagabonding has never been determined by income level; it's found through *simplicity*—the conscious decision of how to use what income you have.

And, contrary to popular stereotypes, seeking simplicity doesn't require that you become a monk, a subsistence forager, or a wild-eyed revolutionary. Nor does it mean that you must unconditionally avoid the role of consumer. Rather, simplicity merely requires a bit of personal sacrifice: an adjustment of your habits and routines within consumer society itself.

At times, the biggest challenge in embracing simplicity will be the vague feeling of isolation that comes with it, since private sacrifice doesn't garner much attention in the frenetic world of mass culture.

> Our crude civilization engenders a multitude of wants. . . . Our forefathers forged chains of duty and habit, which bind us notwithstanding our boasted freedom, and we ourselves in desperation, add link to link, groaning and making medicinal laws for relief.
>
> —JOHN MUIR, *KINDRED AND RELATED SPIRITS*

Jack Kerouac's legacy as a cultural icon is a good example of this. Arguably the most famous American vagabonder of the twentieth century, Kerouac vividly captured the epiphanies of hand-to-mouth travel in books like *On the Road* and *Lonesome Traveler*. In *The Dharma Bums*, he wrote about the joy of living with people who blissfully ignore "the general demand that they consume production and therefore have to work for the privilege of consuming, all that crap they didn't really want . . . general junk you always see a week later in the garbage anyway, all of [it] impersonal in a system of work, produce, consume."

Despite his observance of material simplicity, however, Kerouac found that his personal life—the life that had afforded him the freedom to travel—was soon overshadowed by a more fashionable (and marketable) public vision of his travel life*style*. Convertible cars, jazz records, marijuana—and, later, Gap khakis—ultimately came to represent the mystical "It" that he and Neal Cassady sought in *On the Road*. As his Beat cohort William S. Burroughs was to point out years after Jack's death, part of Kerouac's mystique became inseparable from the idea that he "opened a million coffee bars and sold a million pairs of Levi's to both sexes."

In some ways, of course, coffee bars, convertibles, and marijuana are all part of what made travel appealing to Kerouac's readers. That's how marketing (intentional and otherwise) works. But these aren't the things that made travel *possible* for Kerouac. What made travel possible was that he knew how neither self nor wealth can be measured in terms of what you consume or own. Even the downtrodden souls on the fringes of society, he observed, had something the rich didn't: time.

This notion—the notion that "riches" don't necessarily make you wealthy—is as old as society itself. The ancient Hindu Upanishads refer disdainfully to "that chain of possessions wherewith men bind themselves, and beneath which they sink"; ancient Hebrew scriptures declare that "whoever loves money never has money enough." Jesus noted that it's pointless for a man to "gain the whole world, yet lose his very self," and the Buddha whimsically pointed out that seeking happiness in one's material desires is as absurd as "suffering because a banana tree will not bear mangoes."

Despite several millennia of such warnings, however, there is still an overwhelming social compulsion—an insanity of consensus, if you will—to get rich from life rather than live richly, to "do well" in the world instead of living well. And, in spite of the fact that America is famous for its unhappy rich people, most of us remain convinced that just a little more money will set life right. In this way, the messianic metaphor of modern life becomes the lottery—that outside chance that the right odds will come together to liberate us from financial worries once and for all.

Fortunately, we were all born with winning tickets—

and cashing them in is a simple matter of altering our cadence as we walk through the world. Vagabonding sage Ed Buryn knew as much: "By switching to a new game, which in this case involves vagabonding, time becomes the only possession and everyone is equally rich in it by biological inheritance. Money, of course, is still needed to survive, but *time* is what you need to live. So, save what little money you possess to meet basic survival requirements, but spend your time lavishly in order to create the life values that make the fire worth the candle. Dig?"

> Henceforth I ask not good-fortune, I myself am good-fortune,
> Henceforth I whimper no more, postpone no more, need nothing.
>
> —WALT WHITMAN, "SONG OF THE OPEN ROAD"

Dug. And the best part is that, as you cultivate your future with rich fields of time, you are also sowing the seeds of personal growth that will gradually bloom as you travel into the world.

In a way, simplifying your life for vagabonding is easier than it sounds. This is because travel by its very nature demands simplicity. If you don't believe it, just go home and try stuffing everything you own into a backpack. This will never work, because no matter how meagerly you live at home, you can't match the scaled-down min-imalism that travel requires. You can, however, set the process of reduction and simplification into motion while you're still at home. This is useful on several lev-els: Not only does it help you to save up travel money, but it helps you realize how independent you are of your possessions and your routines. In this way, it prepares you mentally for the realities of the road, and makes travel a dynamic extension of the life-alterations you began at home.

As with, say, giving up coffee, simplifying your life will require a somewhat difficult consumer withdrawal period. Fortunately, your impending travel experience will give you a very tangible and rewarding long-term goal that helps ease the discomfort. Over time, as you reap the sublime rewards of simplicity, you'll begin to wonder how you ever put up with such a cluttered life in the first place.

> Travel can be a kind of monasticism on the move: On the road, we often live more simply, with no more possessions than we can carry, and surrendering ourselves to chance. This is what Camus meant when he said that "what gives value to travel is fear"—disruption, in other words (or emancipation), from circumstance, and all the habits behind which we hide.
>
> —PICO IYER, "WHY WE TRAVEL"

On a basic level, there are three general methods to simplifying your life: stopping expansion, reining in your routine, and reducing clutter. The easiest part of this process is stopping expansion. This means that in anticipation of vagabonding, you don't add any new possessions to your life, regardless of how tempting they might seem. Naturally, this rule applies to things like cars and home entertainment systems, but it also applies to travel accessories. Indeed, one of the biggest mistakes people make in anticipation of vagabonding is to indulge in a vicarious travel buzz by investing in water filters, sleeping bags, and travel-boutique wardrobes. In reality, vagabonding runs smoothest on a bare minimum of gear—and even multiyear trips require little initial investment beyond sturdy footwear and a dependable travel bag or backpack.

While you're curbing the material expansion of your life, you should also take pains to rein in the unnecessary expenses of your weekly routine. Simply put, this means living more humbly (even if you aren't humble) and investing the difference into your travel fund. Instead of eating at restaurants, for instance, cook at home and pack a lunch for work or school. Instead of partying at nightclubs and going out to movies or pubs, entertain at home with friends or family. Wherever you see the chance to eliminate an expensive habit, take it. The money you save as a result will pay handsomely in travel time. In this way, I ate lot of bologna sandwiches (and missed out on a lot of grunge-era Seattle nightlife) while saving up for a vagabonding stint after college—but the ensuing eight months of freedom on the roads of North America more than made up for it.

Perhaps the most challenging step in keeping things simple is reducing clutter—downsizing what you already own. As Thoreau observed, downsizing can be the most vital step in winning the freedom to change your life: "I have in my mind that seemingly wealthy, but most terribly impoverished class of all," he wrote in *Walden*, "who have accumulated dross, but know not how to use it, or get rid of it, and thus have forged their own golden or silver fetters."

How you reduce your "dross" in anticipation of travel will depend on your situation. If you're young, odds are you haven't accumulated enough to hold you down (which, incidentally, is a

> Very many people spend money in ways quite different from those that their natural tastes would enjoin, merely because the respect of their neighbors depends upon their possession of a good car and their ability to give good dinners. As a matter of fact, any man who can obviously afford a car but genuinely prefers travels or a good library will in the end be much more respected than if he behaved exactly like everyone else.
>
> —BERTRAND RUSSELL, *THE CONQUEST OF HAPPINESS*

big reason why so many vagabonders tend to be young). If you're not so young, you can re-create the carefree conditions of youth by jettisoning the things that aren't necessary to your basic well-being. For much of what you own, garage sales and online auctions can do wonders to unclutter your life (and score you an extra bit of cash to boot). Homeowners can win their travel freedom by renting out their houses; those who rent accommodations can sell, store, or lend out the things that might bind them to one place.

An additional consideration in life-simplification is debt. As Laurel Lee wryly observed in *Godspeed,* "Cities are full of those who have been caught in monthly payments for avocado green furniture sets." Thus, if at all possible, don't let avocado green furniture sets (or any other seemingly innocuous indulgence) dictate the course of your life by forcing you into ongoing cycles of production and consumption. If you're already in debt, work your way out of it—and stay out. If you have a mortgage or other long-term debt, devise a situation (such as property rental) that allows you to be independent of its obligations for long periods of time. Being free from debt's burdens simply gives you more vagabonding options.

> It is easy in the world to live after the world's opinion; it is easy in solitude to live after your own; but the great man is he who in the midst of the crowd keeps with perfect sweetness the independence of solitude.
>
> —RALPH WALDO EMERSON, "SELF-RELIANCE"

And, for that matter, more life options.

As you simplify your life and look forward to spending your new wealth of time, you're likely to get a curious reaction from your friends and family. On one level, they will express enthusiasm for your impending adventures. But on another level, they might take your growing freedom as a subtle criticism of their own way of life. Because your fresh worldview might appear to call their own values into question (or, at least, force them to consider those values in a new light), they will tend to write you off as irresponsible and self-indulgent. Let them. As I've said before, vagabonding is not an ideology, a balm for societal ills, or a token of social status. Vagabonding is, was, and always will be a private undertaking—and its goal is to improve your life not in relation to your neighbors but in relation to yourself. Thus, if your neighbors consider your travels foolish, don't waste your time trying to convince them otherwise. Instead, the only sensible reply is to quietly enrich your life with the myriad opportunities that vagabonding provides.

Interestingly, some of the harshest responses I've received in reaction to my vagabonding life have come while traveling. Once, at Armageddon (the site in Israel, not the battle at the end of the world), I met an American aeronautical engineer who was so tickled at having negotiated five days of free time into a Tel Aviv consulting trip that he spoke of little else as we walked through the ruined city. When I eventually mentioned that I'd been traveling around Asia for the past eighteen months, he looked at me as if I'd slapped him. "You must be filthy rich," he said acidly. "Or maybe," he added, giving me the once-over, "your mommy and daddy are."

I tried to explain how two years of teaching English in Korea had funded my freedom, but the engineer would have none of it. Somehow, he couldn't accept that two years of *any* kind of honest work could have funded eighteen months (and counting) of travel. He didn't even bother sticking around for the real kicker: In those eighteen months of travel, my day-to-day costs were significantly *cheaper* than they would have been back in the United States.

The secret to my extraordinary thrift was neither secret nor extraordinary: I had tapped into that vast well of free time simply by forgoing a few comforts as I traveled. Instead of luxury hotels, I slept in clean, basic hostels and guesthouses. Instead of flying from place to place, I took local buses, trains, and share-taxis. Instead of dining at fancy restaurants, I ate food from street vendors and local cafeterias. Occasionally, I traveled on foot, slept out under the stars, and dined for free at the stubborn insistence of local hosts.

In what ultimately amounted to over two years of travel in Asia, eastern Europe, and the Middle East, my lodging averaged out to just under five dollars a night, my meals cost well under a dollar a plate, and my total expenses rarely exceeded one thousand dollars a month.

Granted, I have simple tastes—and I didn't linger long in expensive places—but there was nothing exceptional in the way I traveled. In fact, entire multinational backpacker circuits (not to mention budget-guidebook publishing empires) have been created by the simple abundance of such travel bargains in the developing world. For what it costs to fill your gas tank back home, for example, you can take a train from one end of China to the other. For the price of a home-delivered pepperoni pizza, you can eat great meals for a

> When I was very young a big financier once asked me what I would like to do, and I said, "To travel." "Ah," he said, "it is very expensive; one must have a lot of money to do that." He was wrong. For there are two kinds of travelers; the Comfortable Voyager, round whom a cloud of voracious expenses hums all the time, and the man who shifts for himself and enjoys the little discomforts as a change from life's routine.
>
> —RALPH BAGNOLD, *LIBYAN SANDS*

week in Brazil. And for a month's rent in any major American city, you can spend a year in a beach hut in Indonesia. Moreover, even the industrialized parts of the world host enough hostel networks, bulk transportation discounts, and camping opportunities to make long-term travel affordable.

Ultimately, you may well discover that vagabonding on the cheap becomes your favorite way to travel, even if given more expensive options. Indeed, not only does simplicity save you money and buy you time; it also makes you more adventuresome, forces you into sincere contact with locals, and allows you the independence to follow your passions and curiosities down exciting new roads.

In this way, simplicity—both at home and on the road—affords you the time to seek renewed meaning in an oft-neglected commodity that can't be bought at any price: life itself.

Tip Sheet

RESOURCES FOR LIFESTYLE SIMPLICITY

Your Money or Your Life: Transforming Your Relationship with Money and Achieving Financial Independence, by Joe Dominguez and Vicki Robin (Penguin USA, 1999)
This bestselling book uses a nine-step process to demonstrate how most people are making a "dying" instead of a living. Includes practical pointers for achieving financial independence by altering your lifestyle.

Voluntary Simplicity: Toward a Way of Life That Is Outwardly Simple, Inwardly Rich, by Duane Elgin (Quill, 1993)

First published in 1981, this is a popular reference and inspiration for those looking to live a simpler life. Strongly themed toward environmental sustainability.

The Simple Living Guide: A Sourcebook for Less Stressful, More Joyful Living, by Janet Luhrs (Broadway Books, 1997)
Luhrs is the founder and publisher of the Simple Living Journal *(companion website at http://www.simpleliving .com/). The book contains tips for living fully and well through simplicity.*

Less Is More: The Art of Voluntary Poverty—an Anthology of Ancient and Modern Voices Raised in Praise of Simplicity, edited by Goldian Vandenbroeck (Inner Traditions, 1996)
Quotes and essays on the value of simplicity, from the likes of Socrates, Shakespeare, Saint Francis, Benjamin Franklin, and Mohandas Gandhi, as well as the Bible, The Dhammapada, Tao Te Ching, *and* The Bhagavad Gita.

Dematerializing: Taming the Power of Possessions, by Jane Hammerslough (Perseus Books, 2001)
An examination of "possession-obsession" and how it negatively affects our personal growth, creativity, and relationships.

Walden, by Henry David Thoreau
The philosophical account of Thoreau's experiment in antimaterialist living. An American literary classic for over 150 years.

BUDGETING AND MONEY MANAGEMENT

The Pocket Idiot's Guide to Living on a Budget, by Peter J. Sander and Jennifer Basye Sander (Alpha Books, 1999)
A concise guide to planning and abiding by a day-to-day budget.

The Budget Kit: The Common Cents Money Management Workbook, by Judy Lawrence (Dearborn Trade, 2000)
Easy-to-use tips for managing your finances and getting the most out of your income.

The Complete Tightwad Gazette: Promoting Thrift as a Viable Alternative Lifestyle, by Amy Dacyczyn (Random House, 1999)
Nine hundred pages of tips for frugal living.

The Dollar Stretcher (http://www.stretcher.com/)
An online resource for saving money in day-to-day life. Features weekly columns on thrift and simplicity.

VAGABONDING FOR SENIORS AND FAMILIES

Statistically, most vagabonders are eighteen to thirty-five years old and childless—but this doesn't mean that youthful independence is a prerequisite for long-term travel. Indeed, some of the most dynamic vagabonders are the adventurous elder and family travelers who defy stereotype and set out to discover the world for themselves.

Senior Vagabonders

On a general level, all of the advice in this book—from choosing a guidebook to interacting with local cultures—applies just as readily to older travelers as to younger ones. Senior vagabonders might occasionally seek out more creature comforts than their younger counterparts, but the same basic rules and freedoms of independent travel apply. And since most cultures treat elders with uncommon interest and respect, older travelers invariably wander into charming adventures and friendships on the road. Naturally, extra care should be taken in tourist zones (see chapter 6), where unscrupulous touts and scam artists often see seniors as easy marks.

Some older vagabonders might feel a little intimidated at the outset of their travels, since independent travel is often cast in a youth-culture vernacular. One way to offset this anxiety is to join up with a brief package tour or "volunteer vacation" program at the outset of your journey. Given a good attitude and a proper level of awareness, you'll feel much more confident about independent travel after these initial days or weeks in your host culture.

Travel Unlimited: Uncommon Adventures for the Mature Traveler, by Alison Gardner (Avalon Travel Publishing, 2000)
A worldwide menu of active travel opportunities for the older adventurer. The book emphasizes "vacation" travel but is a good starting point for seniors wanting to know about alternative travel opportunities, including volunteering and "eco-tourism."

Marco Polo Magazine
"Dedicated to adventure travelers over fifty." Features down-to-earth articles about older travelers making their own way on the road; $10 for a four-issue (one-year) sub-

scription. *Companion website at http://www.marcopolo magazine.com.*

Elderhostel
The world's largest educational and travel organization for adults fifty-five and over. Offers ten thousand programs a year in over one hundred countries. A good way for traveling seniors to get a taste of other cultures before striking off on their own. Information online at http://elderhostel.org.

State Department Travel Tips for Older Americans
Posted online (http://travel.state.gov/olderamericans .html), this tip sheet is a useful primer for older independent travelers. Topics covered include trip preparation, passport and visas, health, money and valuables, safety precautions, and shopping.

Vagabonding with Children

Parenthood may be an adventure in and of itself, but this doesn't mean that you have to limit the adventure to your hometown. For children of any age (and six- to fourteen-year-olds in particular), an extended journey into the world can be an unparalleled educational experience that inspires new interests and passions. And while the task of parenting on the road can sometimes be a challenge for the grown-ups, the singular adventures (and collective memories) of family vagabonding will more than make up for it.

Lonely Planet Travel with Children, by Cathy Lanigan and Maureen Wheeler (Lonely Planet, 2002)

A practical guide to the challenges and joys of traveling with children, including trip preparation and kid-friendly destinations.

Gutsy Mamas: Travel Tips and Wisdom for Mothers on the Road, by Marybeth Bond (Travelers' Tales, 1997)
Inspirational and informative advice on staying healthy on the road, traveling to Third World countries (and close to home), and keeping children of all ages entertained and adults energized.

Your Child's Health Abroad, by Jane Wilson-Howarth and Matthew Ellis (Bradt Publications, 1998)
Accessible and practical health information for parents traveling with children to far-flung areas of the world.

One Year Off: Leaving It All Behind for a Round-the-World Journey with Our Children, by David Elliot Cohen (Simon & Schuster, 1999)
When David Elliot Cohen turned forty, he quit his job, sold his house and car, and left to travel the world—with his wife and three kids (ages eight, seven, and two) in tow. A firsthand account of how vagabonding exotic lands can be a family experience.

Worldhop: One Family, One Year, One World (http://www .worldhop.com/)
Online journals and inspiration from an Alaska family (ages forty-nine, forty-eight, fourteen, and seven) who sold and stored their possessions, quit work and school, and spent a year traveling around the world.

Family Travel Forum (http://familytravelforum.com)
Online information on worldwide destinations for adults

and children. Features discussion boards and advice for all manner of family travel issues.

Traveling Internationally with Your Kids
(http://travelwithyourkids.com)
Online resources for traveling overseas with children. Features guidebook recommendations, trip preparation tips, and activity suggestions.

For a fully updated and linkable online version of this resource guide, surf to http://vagabonding.net/ and follow the "Resources" link.

VAGABONDING VOICES

To allow for travel, we spend less money on things at home (new cars, clothes, stuff in general). We have no debt, including credit card debt—in order to remain financially free to leave. We rent out our home each year when we travel. With no debt (except a mortgage), renting our house allows us to leave without sending a dime back home. Most Americans don't live this way. Their huge debt load would make it awfully difficult to leave. And as an aside, many of our middle-aged friends tell us, "Oh, we'd love to do what you do, but we can't"—money, debt, obligations, etc. The way I see it is that most folks simply choose their boxes. Any of us do what is fundamentally most important to us.

—LINDA ROSE, 58,
RETIRED TEACHER, OREGON

My lifestyle sacrifices for travel are mainly in relation to American life, which means I still live quite luxuriously. Riding my bike rather than taking the metro or taxis, and packing my lunch rather than spending eight bucks every day, is hardly much of a sacrifice. I try not to buy much meat and coffee and alcohol, but I still go out for those things occasionally. I don't go to the mall and buy clothes. Also, I refuse to spend money on haircuts. It's amazing how much you can save when you don't mind looking like a schmuck for a few months.

—SAM ENGLAND, 25,
STUDENT AND TEMP WORKER,
WASHINGTON, D.C.

———

Deal with all material responsibilities of home before you go on your travels. That way you'll be able to enjoy the experience more fully, not worrying about when exactly you have to come home, or what you'll have to do when you get there. It is easier to live in the now when all responsibilities are taken care of ahead of time.

—R. J. MOSER, 38,
HOME RENOVATOR, WASHINGTON

Henry David Thoreau

My greatest skill has been to want little.

—HENRY DAVID THOREAU, *WALDEN*

Although Henry David Thoreau never traveled very far outside of New England, he promoted an uncommon view of wealth that is essential to vagabonding. Considering all material possessions beyond basic necessities to be an obstacle to true living, he espoused the idea that wealth is found not in what you own but in how you spend your time. "A man is rich," he wrote in *Walden,* "in proportion to the number of things which he can afford to let alone."

Born in Concord, Massachusetts, in 1817, Thoreau trained as an engineer at Harvard, although he never could pinpoint his true profession. At various times, he called himself a schoolteacher, a surveyor, a farmer, a house painter, a pencil maker, a writer, and "sometimes a poetaster." It is as a writer that he is best remembered—particularly for his book *Walden,* the vivid account of his one-year experiment in antimaterialist living.

At Walden Pond, Thoreau lived in such a way that he only had to work six weeks a year: eating vegetables from his garden and fish from the pond; living in a "tight, light, and clean house" that he built himself; avoiding unnecessary expenses, including fresh meat, fancy clothes, and coffee. This left him with ample time to indulge in the things he loved best: reading, writing, walking, thinking, and observing nature.

In this way—through simplicity—Thoreau was able to find true wealth. "Superfluous wealth can buy superfluities only," he wrote. "Money is not required to buy one necessity of the soul."

CHAPTER 4

Reading old travel books or novels set in faraway places, spinning globes, unfolding maps, playing world music, eating in ethnic restaurants, meeting friends in cafes . . . all these things are part of never-ending travel practice, not unlike doing scales on a piano, shooting free-throws, or meditating.

—PHIL COUSINEAU, *THE ART OF PILGRIMAGE*

Learn, and Keep Learning

One of the best travel parables to come from world history involves a certain Christopher Columbus, who—as we all learned in grade school—sailed the ocean blue in the year 1492. That the legendary Italian navigator ever resolved to seek the East by sailing west says a lot about his gumption, but it also shows that he'd done his homework. Using classic geographical texts written by ancient Greek and Latin authors, as well as a copy of Marco Polo's *Travels,* he had good reason to think his westbound quest for Asia might work.

After his initial voyages proved both promising and perplexing, Columbus's third expedition finally sighted land that was unmistakably continental. Instead of confronting uncertainty, however—instead of wading ashore to verify just what he had found—Columbus rushed back to an outpost on Hispaniola and concocted a triumphant letter to send back to Spain. Rather than using empirical evidence to prove that this was China or India, he went back to the Greek and Latin geographers who'd inspired him in the first place. Quoting passage after passage from the erudite ancients, he confidently concluded that he had at last sighted the elusive Asian mainland.

As any bright eight-year-old will tell you, however, his grand assumption was a good hemisphere off.

The example of Columbus can teach us a couple of vital lessons about vagabonding. First, it shows how doing your pretrip homework—that is, harnessing the knowledge of those who examined the world before you—can lead you to fabulous new horizons. By that same token, however, you will never be able to truly appreciate the unexpected marvels of travel if you rely too heavily on your homework and ignore what is right before your eyes.

Thus, you need to strike a balance between tapping the inspiration that compelled you to hit the road and knowing that nothing short of travel itself can prepare you for the new worlds that await. The reason vagabonding is so appealing is that it promises to show you the destinations and experiences you've dreamed about; but the reason vagabonding is so *addictive* is that, joyfully, you'll never quite find what you dreamed. Indeed, the most vivid travel experiences usually find you by accident, and the qualities that will make you fall in love with a place are rarely the features that took you there.

In this way, vagabonding is not just a process of discovering the world but a way of seeing—an *attitude* that prepares you to find the things you weren't looking for.

> Traveling hopefully into the unknown with a little information: dead reckoning is the way most people live their lives, and the phrase itself seems to sum up human existence.
>
> —PAUL THEROUX, *FRESH AIR FIEND*

The discoveries that come with travel, of course, have long been considered the purest form of education a person can acquire. "The world is a book," goes a saying attributed to Saint Augustine, "and those who do not travel read only one page." Vagabonding is all about delving into the thick plots the world promises, and the more you "read" (so to speak), the better you position yourself to keep reading. However, even if you're stuck on the first paragraph, it's still important to ready yourself for the pages to come. After all, you don't stand to grow much from your travels if you just skim your way through the world at random.

Just how extensively you should prepare yourself before vagabonding is a topic of much debate among travelers. Many experienced vagabonders believe that less preparation is actually better in the long run. The naturalist John Muir used to say that the best way to prepare for a trip was to "throw some tea and bread into an old sack and jump over the back fence." Not only does such bold spontaneity add a spark of adventure to your travels, longtime travelers argue, but it also lessens the kind of prejudices and preconceptions that might jade your experience.

It's important to keep in mind, however, that experienced vagabonders already possess the confidence, faith, and know-how to make such spontaneous travel work. They know how easy the travel basics are, and—using their passions, instincts, and a little local information—they begin their immersion education the moment they touch down at their destinations.

Personally, while I respect the spontaneous approach, I prefer the hum of excitement that comes with carefully preparing at home for the trip to come. And, as Phil Cousineau pointed out in *The Art of Pilgrimage*, I tend to believe that "preparation no more spoils the chance for spontaneity and serendipity than discipline ruins the opportunity for genuine self-expression in sports, acting, or the tea ceremony."

For the first-time vagabonder, of course, preparation is a downright necessity—if for no other reason than to familiarize yourself with the fundamental routines of travel, to learn what wonders and challenges await, and to assuage the fears that inevitably accompany any life-changing new pursuit. The key to preparation is to strike a balance between knowing what's out there and being optimistically ignorant. The gift of the information age, after all, is knowing your *options*—not your destiny—and those people who plan their travels with the idea of eliminating all uncertainty and unpre-

> **It is fatal to know too much at the outset: boredom comes as quickly to the traveler who knows his route as to the novelist who is overcertain of his plot.**
>
> —PAUL THEROUX, *TO THE ENDS OF THE EARTH*

dictability are missing out on the whole point of leaving home in the first place.

The goal of preparation, then, is not knowing exactly where you'll go but being confident nonetheless that you'll get there. This means that your attitude will be more important than your itinerary, and that the simple willingness to improvise is more vital, in the long run, than research.

After all, your very first day on the road—in making travel immediate and real—could very well revolutionize every idea you ever gleaned in the library.

As John Steinbeck wrote in *Travels with Charley,* "Once a journey is designed, equipped, and put in process, a new factor enters and takes over. A trip, a safari, an exploration, is an entity . . . no two are alike. And all plans, safeguards, policing, and coercion are fruitless. We find after years of struggle that we do not take a trip; a trip takes us."

Regardless of how much time you choose to spend in travel planning, the odds are your true preparations began long ago, when you first learned there was a world out there to explore. Over a lifetime, various sources of inspiration—novels, teachers, hobbies—help to stoke the vagabonding urge. Once you've made the determined decision to hit the road, of course, this preparation process focuses and intensifies.

The first place many people turn when planning a trip is traditional media (the kind of information you can find at a library), since it represents such a broad variety of resources. However, a lot of media information—especially day-to-day news—should be approached with a healthy amount of skepticism. This is because so many media outlets (especially television and magazines) are more in the business of competing for your attention than giving you a balanced picture of the world. Real people and places become objectified—made *un*real—as the news media dotes on wars, disasters, elections, celebrities, and sporting events.

Moreover, what qualifies as "travel coverage" in the mainstream news revolves primarily around stunts, tie-ins, and commerce: rich men racing balloons around the world; sci-fi fans driving hundreds of miles to catch the latest *Star Wars* premiere; industry insiders comparing air-travel bargains. Personal, long-term travel rarely gets a mention, unless it relates to something moralistic or vaguely alarming (usually in regard to young people). *Time* magazine in particular has the irksome habit of portraying twenty-something backpackers as drug-addled dimwits.

A good rule of thumb, then, when watching news coverage of other countries, is to think about how the average Hollywood movie exports visions of America to other countries. Just as day-to-day American life is not characterized by car chases, gun battles, and unusually large-breasted women, life overseas is not populated by sinister or melodramatic stereotypes. Rather, it is full of people with values not that much different than your own. Before I went to the Middle East, for example, I'd assumed from media images that Syria was a "rogue state" full of humorless police informants and terrorist training camps. Once I'd drummed up the courage to actually visit Syria, however, this stereotype was shattered by the simple warmth and exuberance of the Arabs, Kurds, and Armenians who lived there. If police informants were indeed trailing my every move in Syria, they witnessed little more than a charming succession of home-cooked dinners, spontaneous neighborhood tours, and tea-shop backgammon games.

Thus, to gain accurate perspective and inspiration for your travels, you need to duck the frenzy of day-to-day news and dig for more relevant sources of information. Fortunately, there are plenty of options: literary travel narratives; specialty magazines covering all manner of travel; English-language foreign newspapers and journals; novels set in distant lands; academic and historical studies of other cultures; foreign-language dictionaries and phrasebooks; maps and atlases; scientific and cultural videos and TV programs; almanacs, encyclopedias, and travel reference books; travelogues and guidebooks.

I've listed starting points for various such resources at the end of this chapter, but I'll elaborate a bit here on travel guidebooks, since they're particularly important. Guidebooks should never be your only source of travel information, of course, but they deserve a special mention because they're likely the only resource you'll bring with you on the road. They also contain the kind of pertinent, specialized information that can help even the most timid homebody gain knowledge and courage about the practical possibilities of vagabonding. Nevertheless, you should carefully consider a guidebook's advantages and limitations before you use it to dictate your travels.

> That is the charm of a map. It represents the other side of the horizon where everything is possible.
>
> —ROSITA FORBES, *FROM RED SEA TO BLUE NILE*

Too often, travelers adhere far too religiously to the advice and information that guidebooks dispense. And while some critics blame this trend on the current popularity of "independent" travel guidebooks, this certainly isn't a recent phenomenon. When visiting the Holy Land in the nineteenth century, Mark Twain expressed frequent exasperation at the guidebook fundamentalists in his travel party: "I can almost tell, in set phrase, what they will say when they see Tabor, Nazareth, Jericho, and Jerusalem," Twain wrote in *The Innocents Abroad,* "*because I have the books they will 'smouch' their ideas from.* These authors write pictures and frame rhapsodies, and lesser men follow and see with the author's eyes instead of their own, and speak with his tongue. . . . The pilgrims will tell of Palestine, when they get home, not as it appeared to *them,* but as it appeared in [the guidebooks]—with the tints varied to suit each pilgrim's creed."

Because a guidebook can thus jade your impressions, it's important to use it as a handy reference during your adventures—not as an all-encompassing holy book. Even professional guidebook writers recommend that you maintain a healthy independence from their advice. "There is no need to treat a Lonely Planet book like a bible," travel publisher Tony Wheeler once told me in an interview. "Just because we don't list certain restaurants and hotels doesn't mean they aren't any good. Sometimes people even write to say they use our books only to see where *not* to go. They don't want to stay with everybody else, so they go to the hotels that *aren't* listed in the Lonely Planet. I think that's great because we encourage travelers to be different."

As a general rule, good guidebooks contain useful, condensed travel information relating to a specific region: historical and cultural background; pointers regarding local languages and customs; data on the climate and environment; advice on getting visas and changing money; tips for staying healthy and out of harm's way; instructions for using local transportation; and recommendations for lodging, food, and entertainment. Since owners change and prices are in constant flux, hotel and restaurant recommendations will be the least dependable information in any guidebook you buy. In Vietnam, for example, I found that the hotels and restaurants recommended in the Lonely Planet and the Rough Guide books invariably had the worst customer service, since guidebook notoriety guaranteed them a steady flow of Western travelers. Fortunately, sniffing out comfortable beds and tasty dishes on my own in Vietnam proved to be an easy and enjoyable process once I got a little experience and learned what to look for.

> A good traveler has no fixed plan, and is not intent on arriving.
>
> —LAO-TZU, *THE WAY OF LIFE*

In choosing a guide for your particular destination, it's useful to do a bit of comparison shopping to find the best book for your needs, since guidebook quality tends to vary from country to country. For example, an experienced vagabonder who uses a Moon handbook for Honduras might very well prefer a Bradt guide in Ethiopia, a Lonely Planet guide in Thailand, and a Footprint handbook on the South America circuit. Internet travel message boards and news groups are a good place to inquire about the best guides for your region of choice—though it's important to sample a wide range of opinions, since the guidebook issue occasionally attracts skewed prejudices from travelers.

Since both new and used guidebooks are readily available along most overseas travel circuits, I'd recommend traveling with just one guidebook at a time, regardless of how many regions you plan to visit. It's easy to sell, swap, and buy books as you go, and the weight you save by keeping your books to a minimum will be well worth it. Some vagabonders, in an effort to travel as light as possible, even go so far as to slice out entire portions of their guidebook if they don't plan on using them.

A great alternative to using a guidebook—especially once you've gotten the hang of vagabonding—is to rely instead on an accurate regional map and a language phrasebook. You might miss out on a little contextual information this way, but the quirky destinations and human-centered adventures you'll find in this process will more than make up for it.

In addition to traditional media, there are two useful methods of collecting vagabonding information and inspiration. One method—word of mouth—is the oldest form of intelligence-gathering on the planet. The other method—the Internet—is the newest. Both can enhance your travels, if approached with discernment.

Person-to-person advice is something you'll find most useful once you've started traveling. When you're moving from place to place, it's the best way to relate and reconnoiter travel experiences, sound out new ideas, and get the scoop on the latest prices, warnings, and hot spots in the area you're visiting. Even before you hit the road, it's good to seek advice from like-minded travelers who've gone before you. Salty vagabonders are always happy to share their travel stories, and brimming with enthusiasm at the notion of your impending adventures.

International friends and acquaintances are also great for word-of-mouth advice. If your neighbor hails from Ecuador, quiz him about his homeland; if your coworker is part Bulgarian, ask her about her heritage; if your favorite restaurant is run by Eritreans, ask them if they've heard any news from back home. Odds are, they'll be happy to oblige you with stories and recommendations—and you might even end up with a list of addresses and an admonition to stay with their friends and relatives when you head overseas. I've had enterprising Canadian friends depart on three-month trips to India with more Indian-Canadian contacts than they could hope to visit in three years.

When dealing with any person-to-person travel advice, of course, keep in mind that each individual speaks from his or her own subjective point of view. Thus, be aware that places change with time and circumstance, and that sentimentality and prejudice can cloud memories. Even if someone's description of a place leaves you wonderfully inspired, it never hurts to follow up with concrete research before you go gallivanting off toward some exotic new horizon.

The most dynamic (and, at times, chaotic) travel resource at your disposal is the Internet—which can be seen as an electronic synthesis of traditional media and word-of-mouth information. On one hand, the 'Net is unrivaled in its timeliness and diversity of information; on the other hand, its content is often scatterbrained and self-contradictory. If used with savvy, its resources can inspire you and enable your vagabonding experience in ways no other research tool can. Moreover, it can provide you with an instantaneous vagabonding support community, no matter where you live. It's even possible

> When the virus of restlessness begins to take possession of a wayward man, and the road away from Here seems broad and straight and sweet, the victim must first find in himself a good and sufficient reason for going. This to the practical bum is not difficult. He has a built-in garden of reasons to choose from. Next he must plan his trip in time and space, choose a direction and a destination.
>
> —JOHN STEINBECK, *TRAVELS WITH CHARLEY*

to research and plan all of your travels online, though I certainly wouldn't recommend this.

A great way to dive into the Internet's travel resources is to simply spend an afternoon doing trial-and-error research with a search engine (such as Google or Yahoo!). When surfing the Web for specific information, of course, you will rarely find what you're looking for at the exact moment you're looking for it. However, the countless diversions and false leads of cyberspace can teach you a lot you'd never planned on learning. Thus, patience is a must if your online explorations are going to take you anywhere.

Gradually, you will discover the broad array of travel resources available online: Internet-based travel 'zines; literary and amateur travelogues; online travel and ticketing agencies; regional travel home pages operated by travel hobbyists; travel-related news groups and message boards; online editions of English-language overseas newspapers; resource sites operated by traditional guidebook publishers; online travel sections from major print newspapers and magazines; commercial tour sites; official national and regional tourist information sites; budget travel resource pages and chat rooms; international city guides created and maintained by expatriates; Q & A or FAQ pages run by online "travel gurus"; government travel and health advisories; "responsible travel" guides posted by nonprofit organizations; online bookstores that specialize in travel; and international university research databases covering

> Before the development of tourism, travel was conceived to be like study, and its fruits were considered to be the adornment of the mind and the formation of the judgement. The traveler was a student of what he sought.
>
> —PAUL FUSSELL, *ABROAD*

everything from anthropology to economics to marine biology.

For the first-time vagabonder, online travelogues are a particularly inspiring resource. Though not always filled with flawless prose, these nonprofessional travel diaries help to demystify the road, and they often speak with an honest, unjaded exuberance that is fun to relate to. Furthermore, since online travelogues have been written by vagabonders from nearly every demographic—students, retirees, couples taking two-year honeymoons, parents taking a year off to travel with young children, physically disabled adventurers—they prove that you don't necessarily have to be young, white, and unattached to go vagabonding.

Online message boards and news groups, which give you the opportunity to ask and answer travel-related questions, are also a particularly useful vagabonding resource. Various Usenet news groups within the rec.travel and soc.culture domains are great for tracking down information on specific countries, and many online travel sites (Lonely Planet's Thorn Tree is a particularly popular example) contain message boards relating to all manner of travel. A few tips on using these online bulletin boards: First, be sure to read through all the message threads before you post your question, since there's a good chance it may already have been answered. Second, seek as broad a range of responses as possible, since these postings tend to be anonymous, subjective, and largely unverifiable. And, lastly, keep in mind that the anonymity of these message boards inspires some people to exaggerated levels of nastiness. Before I traveled across Asia, for instance, the Lonely Planet Thorn Tree had me convinced that the entire continent was full of puritanical travel snobs—when in actuality most of the Asia-circuit travelers I came to meet on the road were easygoing and fair-minded.

An additional perk of Internet research is that you can take it on the road with you. By this, I don't mean that you should pack along a laptop computer, but that you should take advantage of the many Internet cafés opening up in all corners of the world. Usually created by area entrepreneurs to give locals (who typically can't afford their own computers) a chance to tap into the on-line world, these storefront computer rooms can be found in most every country in the world and are a great, inexpensive place to catch up on news and seek out new information.

The only caveat here is that you should moderate the amount of time you spend online as you travel—since nothing stifles your vagabonding flexibility quite like the compulsive urge to stay connected to the modern world. Indeed, the surest way to miss out on the genuine experience of a foreign place—the psychic equivalent of trapping yourself back at home—is to obsessively check your e-mail as you travel from place to place.

Travel Preparation Q & A

As you prepare for your travels, you'll find yourself pondering the kinds of practical issues all vagabonders have to face before they hit the road: health needs and immunization requirements; safety issues and travel advisories; passport and visa details; insurance and emergency communication needs; and concerns about food, lodging, and transportation in faraway destinations. Fortunately, a good guidebook will cover most of these issues for your specific destination—though it's always good to double-check timely matters (including visa requirements and travel advisories) on the Internet. I've also listed several trip-preparation resources in the tip sheet at the end of this chapter.

If in doubt about how exactly you will deal with the unexpected over the long haul, remember that simple awareness and adaptation will count for more than detailed troubleshooting. It's hard to predict when or if crime will occur, for instance, but it's easy to maintain habits (such as keeping your cash in a money belt, or always locking up your bag) that will lessen your chances of becoming a victim. In the end, the "worst-case scenarios" you dream up in the planning stage rarely come true. And in the event that some debacle should overtake you on your travels, awareness and adaptation are *still* your best resources.

In addition to these sundry travel preparation matters, most people ponder a few big, basic concerns in anticipation of vagabonding. These concerns include:

The world is a big place. Where should I go?

This could be the hardest question of them all—not because some destinations are necessarily better than others but because all destinations are potentially wonderful in their own way. In essence, choosing one region to explore means forsaking (for the time being, at least) dozens of other fantastic parts of the world. Looking for a conclusive reason to pick one place over another can be maddening.

Fortunately, you don't ever need a really good reason to go anywhere; rather, go to a place for whatever happens when you get there. And as cheeky as that may sound, it's the way vagabonding usually works. You might start a Middle East loop in Egypt because of the

Pyramids, for example, and end up staying there three extra months for completely unrelated reasons (Arabic poetry; belly-dancing lessons; or a desert love affair with a Hungarian archaeologist).

For Americans, the European circuit is an instinctive vagabonding destination, but nearly any part of the world can be travel-friendly. Should you want to get the most out of your travel dollar, Southeast Asia, the Indian subcontinent, the Middle East, Central America, and South America are all home to cheap, safe, time-honored vagabonding circuits. Africa and Oceania (including Australia) are slightly more spendy—but still no more expensive than your average week at home. Even North America (where I did my very first vagabonding stint) can make for a fantastic and affordable long-term travel experience, given the right amount of initiative and thrift.

Of course, the traditional circuits of the budget travel world need only be a mental reference point in planning your travels; your actual vagabonding strategy can (and should) be as conventional or as esoteric as you want it to be. Thus, feel free to draw any inspiration, no matter how stolid or silly, when considering where to go. The fanciful idea of learning to tango, for instance, might make you consider visiting Argentina. A childhood fascination with Mutual of Omaha's *Wild Kingdom* might inspire you to seek out the beasts of Botswana. Perhaps reading Kerouac's *On the Road* will make you want to strike out and see America.

An interest in table tennis might take you to China; a rugby addiction might send you to New Zealand or Fiji. The legend of Prester John might lure you to Ethiopia; a passion for butterflies might send you to Costa Rica; a surfing yen might land you in Australia. A curiosity about your ancestry might call you back to Scotland, the Philippines, or Cuba. Maybe your mother's European hitchhiking trip in the late seventies will inspire you to follow in her footsteps. Maybe you'll head to Singapore just to see how it measures up to the Tom Waits song of the same name. Maybe you'll hit Djibouti simply because the mention of this country made you giggle in junior high geography class. There's even an outside chance that the Taj Mahal snow globe you've cherished since childhood will prompt you to visit India.

Whatever the original motivation for going someplace, remember that you'll rarely get what you expect when you go there—and this is almost always a good thing. While vagabonding through eastern Europe, for instance, I went to Latvia simply because it sounded like a nice, dull place to get some reading and writing done. As it turned out, the parks, cinemas, and kitschy heavy-metal nightclubs of Riga (as well as the friendliness of Latvians in general) kept me there for three lively weeks.

Once you've chosen a vagabonding region, don't get too ambitious just yet about what you want to do there. For all you've studied and anticipated about a place, you'll find twenty times more after a few days of experiencing it. Thus, go ahead and research a general itinerary—but only so you can estimate your budget and learn what's out there. Don't plan to "do" Asia in six months; instead, aim to see a part of it, like the northeast, the southeast, or India. Similarly, don't plan to "do" Central America in six weeks; you'll have a much more vivid experience if you limit yourself to a country or two. And—even if you have two years to play with—trying to cram five continents into a single vagabonding stint is a sure path to jadedness and exhaustion. Vagabonding is not like bulk shopping: The value of your travels does not hinge on how many stamps you have in your passport when you get home—and the slow, nuanced experience of a single country is always better than the hurried, superficial experience of forty countries.

Moreover, resist the temptation to purchase your specifics in advance. Indeed, as wonderful as that Ugandan safari looks in the promotional literature of a Dallas-based travel company, shopping for the same experience when you arrive in Africa will be infinitely less expensive—and you'll have saved yourself the trouble of adhering to a fixed date. The same goes for air travel. Despite how tempting a discounted "around-the-world" flight ticket might seem, it's generally better to buy a one-way ticket to your first destination and plan your ongoing transportation as you go. Not only is it cheaper this way (thanks to frumpy local airlines such as Biman Bangladesh, Aerocaribbean, and Malev Air) but it allows you a more organic experience, since you'll have a much better feel for your travels en route than you will before they begin.

Accordingly, there's no need to prearrange all of your national entry visas before you leave, since these are easy to acquire en route (and thus less likely to expire or become useless when your plans change). This in mind, pack a dozen or so visa-sized photos of yourself, just to avoid the hassle of getting mug shots overseas. Check the visa requirements of your *initial* destination before you leave, of course, since many popular countries (such as China and India) still don't issue visas on arrival.

As a general rule, remember that prepackaged adventures and specific arrangements—even those touted under the guise of "budget travel"—are for people who can spare only a couple of weeks away from home. Vagabonding is about setting your own pace and finding your own way, and you can rest assured that everything you see in a glossy brochure in Milwaukee will be just as available (and ten times cheaper) when you arrive independently at your destination.

Should I plan to travel alone or with a companion?

There is no universal answer to this question, since it's ultimately a matter of personal preference. I've traveled both ways, and found both enjoyable. For my first vagabonding trip (eight months around North America), traveling with friends allowed me to share the challenges and triumphs of travel and, by splitting costs, helped me save money. The team dynamic also made it easier to overcome my anxieties and hit the road in the first place. All of my ensuing vagabonding journeys, however, have been solo—which I've found is a great way to immerse myself in my surroundings. Without a partner, I have complete independence, which inspires me to meet people and find experiences that I normally wouldn't have sought. Plus, going solo is never a strict modus operandi for me: whenever I tire of solitude, it's always easy to hook up with other travelers for a few days or weeks as I go.

If you'd prefer to travel with a partner from the outset, be sure to choose your company wisely. Make certain that you share similar goals and ideas about how you want to travel. If your idea of a constructive afternoon in Cambodia is, say, identifying flora on the jungle floor, you probably shouldn't pick a partner who'd prefer a seedy bar and a half dozen hookers. If possible, go on short road trips with your potential partner before you go vagabonding together; it's amazing what you can learn about your compatibility in just a couple of days. Avoid compulsive whiners, chronic pessimists, mindless bleeding hearts, and self-conscious hipsters, since these kinds of people (who are surprisingly common along the travel trail) have a way of turning travel into a tiresome farce. Instead, find a partner who exudes an attitude of realism and open-mindedness (see chapter 8); these are the virtues you yourself will want to cultivate.

Regardless of how compatible you are with your companion—even if your companion is a lover, sibling, or spouse—have no illusions about spending every moment together. Perfect harmony on the road is a pipe dream, so always allow your partnership room to breathe, even if this means amicably splitting up for weeks at a time. Thus, in your mental as well as your practical preparations, you should always be ready to go it alone—even if you don't think you'll have to.

What should I plan to bring on my travels?

As little as possible, period. I can't emphasize enough how important it is to travel light. Dragging an enormous pack full of junk from place to place is the surest way to hamstring your flexibility and turn your travels into a ridiculous, grunting charade.

Unfortunately, life at home can't prepare you for how little you need on the road. Even people who think they're adhering to bare survival necessities when packing at home generally end up dumping three-quarters of their junk within two weeks on the road. Thus, the biggest favor you can do for yourself when trying to decide what to bring is to buy—and this is no joke—a very small travel bag.

This small pack, of course, will allow you only the minimum: a guidebook, a pair of sandals, standard hygiene items, a few relevant medicines (including sunscreen), disposable earplugs (for those inevitable noisy environments), and some small gift items for your future hosts and friends. Add a few changes of simple, func-tional clothes and one somewhat nice outfit for customs checks and social occasions. Toss in a good pocketknife, a small flashlight, a decent pair of sunglasses, a day pack (for carrying smaller items when you leave your hotel or guesthouse), and an inexpensive camera. And then—looking down to make sure you have a sturdy pair of boots or walking shoes on your feet—close the bag and affix a small, strong padlock.

This might seem like a shockingly scant amount of travel gear, but not if you consider that you will be trav-eling into a world of people who have pretty much the same day-to-day needs as you do. Indeed, wherever you go in the world, you will find plenty of toiletries, extra clothes, pens, notebooks, tissues, towels, bottled water, and snacks—even if the brand names don't seem all that familiar. Any place that is rainy will have plenty of cheap umbrellas for sale; mosquito nets will be easily found in areas with lots of insects; warm clothes (some of them charmingly ethnic) are sure to be sold anyplace where the weather gets cold. And shopping for such supplies as you need them can be an adventure in itself. As for rele-vant books and maps, they're often easier to find (even in their English edition) at your destination than at home.

Camping equipment is something you should bring only if you're certain you will use it on a *frequent basis*. Unless you have specifically planned a large portion of your trip in the backcountry (or if, in some North Amer-ican and western European areas, camping is the only affordable way to experience your destination), don't bring a tent, a sleeping bag, or cooking gear while vagabonding. Should you feel the urge to sleep rough from time to time, locally purchased hammocks or inex-pensive blankets can do wonders. Even in rugged places like the Andes or the Himalayas, it's generally easier to rent quality equipment (and guides) than to haul in your own trekking gear.

All expensive items, such as jewelry and electronics, should be left at home. This includes laptop computers and high-performance digital cameras, since these items tend to get stolen or broken and (unless you're a professional-class writer or photographer) ballpoint pens, Internet cafés, and point-and-shoot cameras can meet your needs just as well. If you feel you can't survive without occasionally saving text files or using your favorite software as you travel, bring your own disks or CD-ROMs to use in overseas Internet cafés (which, incidentally, are usually set up for Windows instead of Mac OS).

How do I deal with money issues on the road?

A few years ago, a travel friend confidently predicted that "every country with paved runways at its major airports" would soon have automated teller machines in their major urban centers. I don't know that this has happened just yet, but there's no doubt that the increasing availability of ATMs worldwide is making cash management much easier for travelers. Not only do ATMs give a competitive rate of exchange overseas, they also save you the hassle of preparing and carrying all of your travel money at once. ATMs *are* less common outside of industrialized countries, but they are numerous enough that you can find and use them in the bigger cities along your route—thus allowing you to periodically stock up on local currency and save your traveler's checks for more far-flung locations. Before you leave, of course, check with your bank about the overseas compatibility of your ATM card.

As for traveler's checks, you'll invariably get the best

exchange rate from one-hundred-dollar denominations. Be sure to carry a copy of your traveler's check numbers separate from the checks themselves; I generally store these numbers (as well as emergency phone numbers) in a discreet corner of my Web-based e-mail account, just to be safe. Cash dollars are invariably useful when you run out of local currency away from urban areas; it doesn't hurt to stash the bills in various hiding places in your luggage and on your person. Your traveler's checks and passport, of course, should be hidden in a money belt under your clothing.

As for predicting your vagabonding expenses, don't get too hung up on the minute details of budgeting, since you'll have a better feel for things once you're actually traveling. To be safe, keep your cost projections on the conservative side, and don't forget to estimate for visa fees, airport taxes, souvenirs, and occasional "luxury" indulgences (nice hotels, fancy dinners, scuba diving lessons, and the like). If you think you have just enough money to travel for six months, for example, plan on traveling for four months. If you have money remaining after those four months, consider the two (or possibly more) extra months a bonus. As a rule, it's best not to travel your way down to your last dime, even if you plan on getting road jobs from time to time. Set aside a few hundred dollars as an emergency fund—and resist the urge to find "emergencies" at carpet bazaars and full-moon parties.

Before you leave on your trip, pay all your bills in advance and settle all your debts, so you don't have to worry about these things on the road. Entrust your mail and home financial dealings to a trusted friend or family member, and be sure to give them backup copies of your traveler's checks and passport information. Don't make things too complicated for this person (they're doing you a big favor, after all), and be sure to leave clear instructions about what to do in possible emergency scenarios. Of course, you should handsomely reward this person with exotic gifts once you've returned from your travels.

The transition from home life to vagabonding seems like such a big step. How do I deal with it?

Never underestimate your ability to learn and adapt quickly—and don't waste your time fretting about every possibility that might come your way on the road. Again, simple courage is worth far more than detailed logistics, and a confident, positive, ready-to-learn attitude will make up for any travel savvy you lack at the outset.

With such an attitude, most people find themselves brimming with confidence after their first few days of vagabonding—and kicking themselves for not having mustered the courage to do it years ago.

Tip Sheet

ONLINE TRAVEL RESEARCH PORTALS

Johnny Jet (http://www.johnnyjet.com)
This Internet travel page is little more than a listing of links, but it's probably the most relevant and well-organized list of topical travel resources online. Links to information about air travel, weather, money, travel warnings, insurance, packing, guidebooks, and dozens of other specialty topics.

BootsnAll.com (http://www.bootsnall.com)
Billed as "the ultimate resource for the independent traveler," this online travel community features trip-planning

advice, advice from regional "insiders," a useful message board to post and answer travel questions, and a fine collection of travelogues from everyday vagabonders. A recommended resource for planning and researching your travels.

I Go U Go (http://www.igougo.com)
Another dynamic online travel community, featuring message boards, photo galleries, and "travel journals" from over two thousand destinations worldwide.

Travel-Library.com (http://travel-library.com)
One of the oldest homegrown travel sites on the Internet. Features travel news, destination guides, travel advice, links, and one of the best collections of personal travelogues online. A good starting point for general trip research.

WorldSkip.com (http://www.worldskip.com)
News, information, products, and services from every nation on earth. Excellent country-by-country tip sheets that link to relevant local newspapers and magazines, arts and music sites, tourism tips, economic statistics, and cultural information. A great starting point for specific research on a country.

World Travel Guide (http://wtgonline.com)
Basic travel information on destinations worldwide, including city and country guides that you can download to a handheld computer.

GENERAL TRAVEL PLANNING GUIDES ONLINE

How to See the World: Art of Travel (http://www.art
oftravel.com)
*Twenty-five well-organized chapters about all aspects of
budget travel, including passports, visas, accommodations, transportation, hitchhiking, and equipment.*

Round-the-World Travel Guide (http://travel-library.com/
rtw/html/faq.html)
*A popular section within Travel-Library.com, this online
guidebook was originally written by vagabonder Mark
Brosius, then updated with suggestions from travel-news-
group participants. In addition to sound travel advice, it
contains good tips on financial planning, as well as information about practical considerations you must attend to
before you leave home.*

Vagabond Globetrotting (http://www.mendicott.com/
vgconten.htm)
*A full online version of Marcus Endicott's 1989 travel
guidebook, including tips on money, gear, food, transport,
health, accommodations, and overseas work opportunities. Introduction by Ed Buryn.*

ONLINE GOVERNMENT TRAVEL RESOURCES

Bureau of Consular Affairs, U.S. State Department (http:
//travel.state.gov)
Link page of official travel information for U.S. citizens.

Canadian Consular Affairs (http://www.voyage.gc.ca/
consular_home-e.htm)

Link page of official travel information for Canadian citizens.

Passport Services, U.S. State Department (http://travel
.state.gov/passport__services.html)
*Everything Americans need to know about applying for
and receiving a passport.*

Canadian Passport Office (http://www.dfait-maeci.gc
.ca/passport/howto__e.asp)
*Everything Canadians need to know about applying for
and receiving a passport.*

Foreign Entry Requirements (http://travel.state.gov/
foreignentryreqs.html)
*A U.S. State Department tip sheet listing entry and visa
requirements for Americans traveling to nations worldwide.*

Your Trip Abroad (http://travel.state.gov/yourtrip
abroad.html)
*An extremely basic tip sheet from the U.S. State Depart-
ment listing passport and visa needs, immunization tips,
health and money matters, safety information, and general pointers.*

CIA World Factbook (http://www.odci.gov/cia/publica
tions/factbook)
*A database of basic political, geographical, demographic,
economic, communication, transportation, military, and
transnational statistics about every country in the world.*

GUIDEBOOK PUBLISHERS

Lonely Planet Publications (http://www.lonelyplanet.com)
Australia-based Lonely Planet is the biggest and most well-known franchise in the budget-travel world. These well-researched and well-organized travel guidebooks cover every region of the world; the series also includes language phrasebooks, trekking guides, wildlife-viewing guides, travel-health guides, international-food guides, maps, atlases, and travel videos. The Lonely Planet website is a great portal for travel research, with basic tip sheets for every country in the world, columns from travel experts, an online health guide, "theme guides" to give you travel ideas, international news, and the massive Thorn Tree message board, where you can post and answer questions about all manner of travel.

Moon Handbooks (http://www.moon.com)
Based in the United States, Moon Handbooks are an excellent resource for destinations in North America, Mexico, Central America, and some Asian regions (including Southeast Asia and South Korea; especially useful is the authoritative Indonesia Handbook*).*

Let's Go Publications (http://www.letsgo.com)
Updated yearly by Harvard students since 1960, Let's Go guides have a young emphasis and address the basics for beginning travelers. Strong on European and North American destinations. Website includes travel articles, links, and a message board for destinations and specialty concerns (such as older travelers, gay and lesbian travelers).

Footprint Handbooks (http://www.footprintbooks.com)
Footprint's South America Handbook *(now in its seventy-eighth edition) has been considered the authoritative in-*

dependent travel guide to the continent since the 1920s. Excellent individual guidebooks for Latin American countries, as well as destinations in Southeast Asia, South Asia, and the Middle East. Emphasis on cultural and historical information. Website includes basic travel tips on all countries and regions covered by Footprints books.

Rough Guides Travel (http://travel.roughguides.com)
England's answer to Lonely Planet, with an emphasis on Europe, Asia, Central America, and North America. In addition to guidebooks, Rough Guides Travel also produces phrasebooks, world-music guides, and reference titles regarding travel health and women's travel. Website includes the Travel Talk message board for questions about destinations worldwide; Travel Journals, contributed to by everyday vagabonders; and Spotlight, featuring articles on various regions of the world.

Bradt Travel Guides (http://www.bradt-travelguides .com)
Literary British guidebooks, with excellent coverage of Africa and South America, as well as unusual destinations like Iraq, the Arctic, and the Falkland Islands.

Travelers' Tales (http://www.travelerstales.com)
This series of destination guidebooks and literary anthologies doesn't give much practical travel advice. Rather, its various volumes are lively collections of stories from travelers (famous and otherwise) worldwide. Good inspirational and informative reading before you start your travels.

TRAVEL IDEA BOOKS

Wild Planet! 1,001 Extraordinary Events for the Inspired Traveler, by Tom Clynes (Visible Ink Press, 1995)
A thorough listing and description of festivals, cultural events, and holidays spanning the globe, from the Swedish Crayfish Festival to Thailand's vegetarian monkey feast.

100 Things to Do Before You Die: Travel Events You Just Can't Miss, by Dave Freeman and Neil Teplica (Taylor Publications, 1999)
More travel-event ideas, from Australia's Nude Night-Surfing Contest to Oklahoma's World Cow-Chip-Throwing Championships. Companion website at http://whatsgoing on.com.

INTERNATIONAL INFORMATION AND NEWS

The Economist (http://economist.com)
This London-based magazine offers the best international reporting of any major English-language newsweekly. Widely available overseas; $129 for a one-year subscription.

World Press Review (http://worldpress.org)
Drawing on newspapers and magazines around the world, this monthly magazine examines international issues often overlooked by the U.S. media; $27 for a one-year subscription. Many articles available online.

World News (http://www.worldnews.com)
A network of online newspapers and radio stations covering all regions of the world.

OnlineNewspapers.com (http://www.onlinenewspapers
.com)
*A database offering quick access to online newspapers
from countries worldwide.*

DailyEarth.com Newspaper Directory (http://www
.dailyearth.com)
*Quick links to online newspapers from countries around
the world.*

INDEPENDENT TRAVEL MAGAZINES

Outpost **Magazine** (http://www.outpostmagazine.com)
*A Toronto-based magazine written by adventurous inde-
pendent travelers; $20 for a one-year (six issues) sub-
scription. Many articles archived online.*

Tales from a Small Planet (http://talesmag.com)
*A homegrown online travel magazine featuring book re-
views, "trip reports," message boards, and resources for
expatriates.*

Wanderlust (http://www.wanderlust.co.uk)
*A United Kingdom–based magazine for the independent
traveler; £21 for a one-year (six issues) subscription.*

World Hum (http://worldhum.com)
*This online magazine features first-person literary travel
tales, comprehensive links to other online travel publications (including newspaper travel sections), and the best
travel-oriented weblog in cyberspace.*

GENERAL TRAVEL MAGAZINES

Condé Nast Traveler (http://www.concierge.com/cn
traveler)
*Well-written stories with a strong emphasis on upscale
and luxury travel; $12 for a one-year (twelve issues) sub-
scription. Website features photos, travel advice columns,
and contests.*

Islands (http://www.islandsmag.com)
*Stories by top writers about travel to the islands of the
world; $20 for a one-year (eight issues) subscription.
Some features archived online.*

National Geographic (http://www.nationalgeographic
.com/ngm)
*This classic, beautifully photographed magazine has prob-
ably inspired more vagabonders from childhood than any
other American magazine in the last hundred or so years.
A one-year (twelve issues) subscription costs $34 and in-
cludes membership to the National Geographic Society.
Interactive website features archived photos and stories,
as well as resource links for international issues.*

National Geographic Adventure (http://www.national
geographic.com/adventure)
*Travel and extreme-sports reporting from America's top
adventure writers; $12 for a one-year (ten issues) sub-
scription. Website includes online features, discussion forums, and travel advisories.*

National Geographic Traveler (http://www.national
geographic.com/traveler)
*Travel stories and tips for North American and world des-
tinations; $15 for a one-year (eight issues) subscription.*

Website contains exclusive online features and discussion forums.

Outside Magazine (http://outsidemag.com)
Travel and adventure writing with an emphasis on outdoor sports; $18 for a one-year (twelve issues) subscription. Website features online articles and advice about travel destinations and gear.

Travel + Leisure (http://www.travelandleisure.com)
An American Express publication with an emphasis on luxury travel. Well-written articles on foreign cultures and destinations; $30 for a one-year (twelve issues) subscription. Travel advice, classifieds, and some features available online. ·

STUDENT TRAVEL RESOURCES

Student World Traveler Magazine (http://studenttravels .com)
A magazine designed to motivate and prepare students to travel around the world. Excellent coverage of relevant travel destinations and issues; $15 for a one-year (twelve issues) subscription. Website contains useful links for student travel research.

Council Travel (http://www.counciltravel.com)
Catering to student travelers since the 1940s. Formed "to help individuals gain understanding, acquire knowledge, and develop skills for living in a globally interdependent and multiculturally diverse world." Discounts, insurance, and help for students wanting to travel, work, volunteer, or study abroad.

Student Travel Association (http://www.statravel.com)
Specializing in travel discounts and overseas work visas for students.

BARGAIN AIR TRAVEL INFORMATION

Fly Cheap, by Kelly Monaghan (Intrepid Traveler, 1999)
Strategies and contacts for saving money on airfares. Monaghan also runs a companion website at http://in trepidtraveler.com.

The Travel Detective: How to Get the Best Service and the Best Deals from Airlines, Hotels, Cruise Ships, and Car Rental Agencies, by Peter Greenberg (Random House, 2001)
An entertaining guide for saving money on travel arrangements, though the emphasis is on vacation (as opposed to long-term) travel. Lots of air-travel advice.

Consolidators: Air Travel's Bargain Basement, by Kelly Monaghan (Intrepid Traveler, 1998)
Consolidators, who unload extra seats for airlines at prices over 50 percent off normal fare, offer great air bargains to travelers. This book contains tips on buying tickets from consolidators, as well as a comprehensive directory of consolidator companies.

Airline Ticket Consolidators and Bucket Shops FAQ (http://hasbrouck.org/faq/)
Online tips on finding cheap air tickets, from air travel "guru" Edward Hasbrouck.

ONLINE AIR-TICKETING SERVICES

Cheap Tickets (http://www.cheaptickets.com)

EconomyTravel.com (http://www.economytravel.com)

Expedia Travel (http://www.expedia.com)

Hotwire (http://www.hotwire.com)

LowestFare.com (http://www.lowestfare.com)

Travelocity.com (http://www.travelocity.com)

OTHER ONLINE AIR-TICKET RESOURCES

Air Hitch (http://www.airhitch.org)
A cheap system for finding last-minute airline seats, primarily to European destinations.

Air Tech (http://www.airtech.com)
Offers a discounted, standby-style FlightPass service for travelers with flexible plans.

Priceline.com (http://www.priceline.com)
Name-your-own-price bidding system for air tickets and other travel services.

SkyAuction.com (http://skyauction.com)
Bid on available air tickets to destinations worldwide.

TRAVEL INSURERS

When looking for a travel-insurance policy, make sure that it covers a long-term journey, not just a short-term vacation. If expanding an existing health-insurance plan, make sure all benefits extend to overseas situations.

Highway to Health, Inc. (http://www.highwaytohealth .com) (888) 243-2358

Insurance Services of America (http://www.overseas health.com) (800) 647-4589

Specialty Risk International, Inc. (SRI) (http://www .specialtyrisk.com) (800) 222-4599

Travel Guard Group, Inc. (http://www.travel-guard.com) (800) 826-4919

Travel Insurance Services (http://www.travelinsure.com) (800) 937-1387

WorldTravelCenter.com (http://www.worldtravelcenter .com) (800) 786-5566

For a fully updated and linkable online version of this resource guide, surf to http://vagabonding.net/ and follow the "Resources" link.

VAGABONDING
VOICES

I remember a conversation with a college professor on the train to Sicily, discussing the need to travel. He said, "You can read everything there is in the world about a place, but there is no substitute for smelling it!" He was right! So make plans, but be happy to abandon them, if need be. Kurt Vonnegut once wrote: "Peculiar travel suggestions are dancing lessons from God." I like that. Do as much research before leaving as possible, but certainly don't let fears keep you away. On a given day, Los Angeles is far more dangerous than anyplace I've traveled. Take normal precautions, use common sense if you have any, and you'll be fine. I've eaten street food everywhere I've gone, and the only time I've ever gotten food poisoning was at a McDonald's in my hometown (no kidding).

—BILL WOLFER, 48,
MUSICIAN, CALIFORNIA

Don't think about it too much. Don't make pro-and-con lists. Pro-and-con lists are nothing but trouble. If you think about it too much, you'll just end up staying home and then someday you'll be telling your grandchildren, "I always wanted to do that" instead of showing them photos of the trips you took and giving them advice on where to go. My family and friends often say to me, "I'm living vicariously through you." Don't ever live vicariously. This is *your* life. Live.

—LAVINIA SPALDING, 32,
TEACHER, ARIZONA

———

Talk to people who have done what you want to do—they love to talk about their experiences and will often be your best resources. Know that there is only so much that you can learn about a place before you just have to go there. Write up an itinerary—even if you don't follow it, your grandmother will feel better (mine did). Practice with maps in your hometown. Learn to relax about getting lost. Use common sense, use caution, but don't let paranoia destroy your trip.

—MARY HILL, 27,
TEACHER, NEBRASKA

Bayard Taylor

I am known to the public not as a poet, the only title I covet, but as one who succeeded in seeing Europe with little money.

—BAYARD TAYLOR, 1852 LETTER TO A FRIEND

Bayard Taylor's lifelong ambition was to capture the American imagination with his poems, but this never quite happened. Instead, Taylor got his notoriety in introducing Americans to the notion that you don't need to be rich to travel overseas.

Born in Pennsylvania in 1825, Taylor resolved at age nineteen to travel across Europe. To save money in procuring his passport, he walked from Pennsylvania to Washington, D.C., departing for Europe with just $140 in his pocket. Through thrift and occasional work on the road, Taylor managed to stretch this sum into two years of travel by avoiding commercial inns, eating at farmers' markets instead of restaurants, and walking everywhere. While studying German in Frankfurt, he lived on just thirty-three cents a day.

In *Views Afoot,* published upon his return, he expressed befuddlement at many of his overprepared fellow travelers, who had little interest in anything save simple comfort and canned guidebook wisdom, "scarcely lifting their eyes to see the real scenes." Interestingly, *Views Afoot* turned into a kind of guidebook itself—fueling a budget-travel tradition that has made vagabonding possible for many generations of American travelers.

Taylor never lost his ambition to write poetry, but the success of *Views Afoot* led him to other wanderings in Africa, India, Japan, the Holy Land, and the Arctic Circle. Finally, in 1874, his publishers honored his literary efforts with a special "Household Edition," in the tradition of the great poets.

The name of this eleven-volume work? *Bayard Taylor's Travels.*

PART **III**

On the Road

CHAPTER 5

Traveler, there is no path
paths are made by walking.

—ANTONIO MACHADO, *CANTORES*

Don't Set Limits

Buddhists believe that we live our everyday lives as if inside an eggshell. Just as an unhatched chicken has few clues about what life is truly like, most of us are only vaguely aware of the greater world that surrounds us. "Excitement and depression, fortune and misfortune, pleasure and pain," wrote Dhammapada scholar Eknath Easwaran, "are storms in a tiny, private, shell-bound realm—which we take to be the whole of existence. Yet we can break out of this shell and enter a new world."

Vagabonding is not Nirvana, of course, but the egg analogy can still apply. In leaving behind the routines and assumptions of home—in taking that resolute first step into the world—you'll find yourself entering a much larger and less constrictive paradigm.

In the planning stages of your travels, this notion might seem daunting. But once you take the plunge and get out on the road, you'll quickly find yourself giddy at how easy and thrilling it all is. Normal experiences (such as ordering food or taking a bus) will suddenly seem extraordinary and full of possibility. All the details of daily life that you ignored back home—the taste of a soft drink, the sound of a radio, the smell of the air—will suddenly seem rich and exotic. Food, fashions, and entertainment will prove delightfully quirky and shockingly cheap. In spite of all your preparation, you will invariably find yourself wanting to know more about the histories and cultures that envelop you. The subtle buzz of the unknown, initially a bit of a fright, will soon prove addictive: Simple trips to the market or the toilet can turn into adventures; simple conversations can lead to charming friendships. Life on the road, you'll soon discover, is far less complicated than what you knew back home—yet intriguingly more complex.

"Travel in general, and vagabonding in particular, produces an awesome density of experience," wrote Ed Buryn, ". . . a cramming together of incidents, impressions and life detail that is both stimulating and exhausting. So much new and different happens to you so frequently, just when you're most sensitive to it. . . . You may be excited, bored, confused, desperate and amazed all in the same happy day."

If there's one key concept to remember amid the excitement of your first days on the road, it's this: Slow down.

Just to underscore the importance of this concept, I'll state it again: SLOW . . . DOWN.

For first-time vagabonders, this can be one of the hardest travel lessons to grasp, since it will seem that there are so many amazing sights and experiences to squeeze in. You must keep in mind, however, that the whole point of long-term travel is having the time to move *deliberately* through the world. Vagabonding is about not merely reallotting a portion of your life for travel but rediscovering the entire concept of time. At home, you're conditioned to get to the point and get things done, to favor goals and efficiency over moment-by-moment distinction. On the road, you learn to improvise your days, take a second look at everything you see, and not obsess over your schedule.

> I don't want to hurry it. That itself is a poisonous twentieth-century attitude. When you want to hurry something, that means you no longer care about it and want to get on to other things.
>
> —ROBERT M. PIRSIG, *ZEN AND THE ART OF MOTORCYCLE MAINTENANCE*

Make a point, then, of easing your way into your travels. Shortly after arriving at your initial destination, find a "beachhead" (be it an actual beach, an urban travelers' ghetto, or an out-of-the-way town) and spend a few days relaxing and acclimating yourself. Don't strike off to "hit all the sights" or actualize all your travel fantasies from the get-go. Stay organized and interested, but don't keep a "things to do" list. Watch and listen to your environment. Take pleasure in small details and differences. Look more and analyze less; take things as they come. Practice your flexibility and patience—and don't decide in advance how long you'll stay in one place or another.

In many ways, this transition into travel can be compared to childhood: Everything you see is new and emotionally affecting, basic tasks like eating and sleeping take on a heightened significance, and entertainment can be found in the simplest curiosities and novelties. "Suddenly you are five years old again," Bill Bryson observed in *Neither Here nor There.* "You can't read anything, you only have the most rudimentary sense of how things work, you can't even reliably cross a street without endangering your life. Your whole existence becomes a series of interesting guesses."

In a certain sense, walking through new places with the instincts of a five-year-old is liberating. No longer are you bound to your past. In living so far away from your home, you'll suddenly find yourself holding a clean slate. There's no better opportunity to break old habits, face latent fears, and test out repressed facets of your personality. Socially, you'll find it easier to be gregarious and open-minded. Mentally, you'll feel engaged and optimistic, newly ready to listen and learn. And, as much as anything, you'll find yourself abuzz with the peculiar feeling that you can choose to go in any direction (literally and figuratively) at any given moment.

When you travel you experience, in a very practical way, the act of rebirth. You confront completely new situations, the day passes more slowly, and on most journeys you don't even understand the language the people speak. . . . You begin to be more accessible to others, because they may be able to help you in difficult situations.

—PAULO COELHO, *THE PILGRIMAGE*

Early on, of course, you're bound to make travel

mistakes. Dubious merchants may swindle you, unfamiliarity with cultural customs may cause you to offend people, and you'll often find yourself wandering lost through strange surroundings. Some travelers go to great pains to avoid these neophyte blunders, but they're actually an important part of the learning experience. As the Koran says, "Did you think you should enter the Garden of Bliss without such trials as came to those who passed before you?" Indeed, everyone starts out as a vagabonding greenhorn, and there's no reason to presume you'll be any different.

One of my early gaffes as a vagabonder happened in Chinese Macao, where I found a small slope of green grass while hiking below the walls of the local Portuguese fortress. Since I'd spent most of that week in the concrete confines of Hong Kong, this parklike swath of grass was too tempting to pass up. Flinging aside my day pack, I sprawled out on the turf to soak in a bit of afternoon sun. Eventually, I noticed that a crowd of locals was staring at me. I waved to them, and they giggled. At first I figured they were just charmed by my happy-go-lucky informality, until an English-speaking student courteously approached me.

"I'm sorry," he said, "but it's not healthy to sit on this grass."

"That's okay," I told him. "Where I come from we do this all the time. It's what parks are made for. A few bugs and some pollen never hurt anyone."

"Yes," said the young man, blushing at my stupidity, "but where I come from, the grass is for dogs to use as a toilet."

I forget my exact response to this startling revelation—but my point is that every vagabonder ends up looking like a tourist dork from time to time. "One of the essential skills for a traveler," noted journalist John

Flinn, "is the ability to make a rather extravagant fool of oneself." Thus, allow yourself to laugh and grow through your mishaps. Not only will you learn new things about yourself and your surroundings in the process, but you'll also get a crash course in the traveler's life (which includes such mundane rituals as bargaining for vegetables, navigating unfamiliar surroundings with a guidebook map, and washing your clothes in the hotelroom sink). Given the proper attitude, you'll find yourself attuned to the new rhythms of the vagabonding life within just a few days.

> But the traveler's world is not the ordinary one, for travel itself, even the most commonplace, is an implicit quest for anomaly.
>
> —PAUL FUSSELL, *ABROAD*

On the road, one of the first questions to haunt beginning travelers is a deceptively simple one: "What are you supposed to *do* from day to day?"

At first blush, this question is rather easy to answer: Statistically, people visiting new places tend to seek out local monuments, museums, ruins, natural wonders, cultural highlights, ethnic villages, markets, restaurants, arts performances, recreation activities, hangouts, and nightlife.

Or, in more vivid terms, you'll start your travels by doing the things that you dreamed about when you were still planning your travels: You will stand in awe of the ancients at places like Stonehenge, Angkor Wat, and Machu Picchu; you'll wander amazed through the exhibits of the Smithsonian, the Louvre, or the Hermitage; you'll stare in reverence at sunrise over the African Serengeti, sunset on the Australian outback, or high noon in the steamy jungles of Borneo; you'll listen, rapt, to the otherworldly whistle of Mongolian throat singers, stare in amazement at the swirl of Turkish Sufis, or stomp along madly to Irish drinking songs. You will shop for Mayan weavings in the markets of Chichicastenango; haggle for damask in the souks of Damascus, or bargain for brocade in the merchant alleyways of Varanasi. You will bungee-jump the canyons of New Zealand, climb the slopes of Kilimanjaro, or windsurf the Sea of Galilee. You will have impassioned one-week love affairs (with natives and fellow travelers alike) along the Adriatic coast of Croatia, the cobbled streets of Havana, or the neon avenues of Tokyo. You will sip cappuccino in the cafés of the Italian Riviera, eat fresh fruit in the Sri Lankan highlands, or stare blissfully into space along the clean blue waters of the Costa Rican coast. You will quaff ouzo all day on the islands of Greece, dance to techno all night on the shores of Goa, or lose a week's sleep in the Carnival madness of Rio de Janeiro.

Collectively, these are the sorts of highlights that link together the various "tourist trails" and "traveler circuits" that crisscross the planet.

Unfortunately, life on the traveler circuit is not an unbroken succession of magical moments and mountaintop experiences—and some sights and activities can get redundant after a while. Moreover, the standard attractions of travel (from the temples of Luxor to the party beaches of the Caribbean) can become so crowded and jaded by their own popularity that it's difficult to truly experience them. Indeed, one of the big clichés of modern travel is the fear of letdown at a place you've always dreamed of visiting. (I recall a *New Yorker* cartoon that featured a man looking at pictures of world-famous destinations in a tourist office. "It all looks so great," he says. "I can't wait to be disappointed!")

In his book *The Tourist*, Dean MacCannell lays out the problem in dry academic terms. "The individual act of sightseeing," he writes, "is probably less important than the ceremonial ratification of authentic attractions as objects of ultimate value. . . . The actual act of communion between the tourist and attraction is less important than the image or the idea of society that the collective act generates."

In other words, tourist attractions are defined by their collective popularity, and that very popularity tends to devalue the individual experience of such attractions.

The current trend of globalization only intensifies this feeling, and this has inspired cultural critics the world over to bemoan how "tainted" the world's tourist draws have become. The "malling over" of the Champs-Elysées, the fast-food restaurants that sit within view of the Sphinx at Giza, and the ready availability of granola in the backpacker haunts of Yunnan have all been used as examples of how tourism is "subsuming cultures." Fortunately, such fears say more about the travel habits of cultural critics than the actual reality of the road. Indeed, you need only wander a few minutes from the Champs-Elysées, the Sphinx, or the backpacker dives of Dali if you want untainted glimpses of Paris, Egypt, or China.

> The practice of soulful travel is to discover the overlapping point between history and everyday life, the way to find the essence of every place, every day: in the markets, small chapels, out-of-the-way parks, craft shops. Curiosity about the extraordinary in the ordinary moves the heart of the traveler intent on seeing behind the veil of tourism.
>
> —PHIL COUSINEAU, *THE ART OF PILGRIMAGE*

Strangely, however, few people (even Lonely Planet–clutching "independent" travelers) think to stray from the accepted travel routes. It's almost as if the tourist trail has become some kind of science-fiction force field—a web of attractions, amenities, and infrastructure from which only intrepid heroes can escape.

Fortunately, finding a singular travel experience doesn't require heroism so much as a simple change of mind-set. The reason so many travelers become frustrated while visiting world-famous destinations is that they are still playing by the rules of home, which "reward" you for following set routines and protocols. Thus, on the road, you should never forget that you are uniquely in control of your own agenda. If the line for Lenin's tomb outside the Kremlin is too long, you have the right to buy a couple bottles of beer, plant yourself at the edge of Red Square, and happily watch the rest of Moscow swirl around you. If Indonesia's Kuta Beach feels too much like a strip mall, you have the right to toss your guidebook aside, take a bus inland, and get lost in the sleepy mountain villages of Bali. If the sight of a McDonald's franchise at the edge of Tiananmen Square bugs you, you have the right to jump on a city bus, get off at random, and wander out to observe everyday life in the ancient *hutongs* of Beijing.

> Bear in mind that the special advantage of vagabonding is the experience of not really knowing what happens next, which you can obtain at bargain rates in all cases. . . . The challenges you face offer no alternative but to cope with them. And in doing that, your life is being fully lived.
>
> —ED BURYN, *VAGABONDING IN EUROPE AND NORTH AFRICA*

Of course, habitual avoidance of the "sights" can be a cliché in itself—especially within the pseudocounterculture crowd that Paul Fussell called "antitourists." "The anti-tourist is not to be confused with the traveler," wrote Fussell in *Abroad*. "His motive is not inquiry but self-protection and vanity." Ostentatiously dressing in local fashions, deliberately not carrying a camera, and "sedulously avoiding the standard sights," the antitourist doesn't have much integrity or agenda beyond his self-conscious decision to stand apart from other tourists.

So endemic is this mentality that many beginning wanderers are looped into the antitourist mind-set from their first day on the road. In the backpacker satire *Are You Experienced?*, pop novelist William Sutcliffe comically portrays a group of young travelers who *can't figure out what to do* while avoiding the tourist mainstream in India. "The most eloquent defense of travel," observes the main character, "was from Paul, who said, 'Dunno. There must be *something* to do. Apparently the dope's really cheap.' "

Indeed, dope *is* cheap in many parts of the world (so long as you aren't caught with it), but this is hardly the secret to keeping yourself interested and impassioned in foreign lands. Rather, the secret to staying intrigued on the road—the secret to truly being different from the frustrated masses—is this: Don't set limits.

Don't set limits on what you can or can't do. Don't set limits on what is or isn't worthy of your time. Dare yourself to "play games" with your day: watch, wait, listen; allow things to happen. Wherever you are, be it the Vatican gift shop, a jungle village in Panama, or downtown Ouagadougou—keep aware of the tiniest tics and details that surround you. As Dean MacCannell pointed out, "*Anything* that is remarked, even little flowers or leaves picked up off the ground and shown to a child, even a shoeshine or gravel pit, *anything* is potentially an attraction. . . . Sometimes we have official guides and travelogues to assist us in this point. Usually we are on our

> "What I find is that you can do almost anything or go almost anywhere, if you're not in a hurry."
>
> —PAUL THEROUX, QUOTING TONY THE BEACHCOMBER, IN *THE HAPPY ISLES OF OCEANIA*

own. How else do we know another person except as an ensemble of suggestions hollowed out from the universe of possible suggestions? How else do we begin to know the world?"

In this way, vagabonding is like a pilgrimage without a specific destination or goal—not a quest for answers so much as a celebration of the questions, an embrace of the ambiguous, and an *openness* to anything that comes your way.

Indeed, if you set off on down the road with specific agendas and goals, you will at best discover the pleasure of actualizing them.

But if you wander with open eyes and simple curiosity, you'll discover a much richer pleasure—the simple feeling of *possibility* that hums from every direction as you move from place to place.

Tip Sheet

GETTING STARTED

• Don't be intimidated by the seemingly intricate details of independent travel. Every major region in the world has independent-travel circuits full of normal travelers just like you. Though you'll eventually want to wander off of these circuits, they naturally provide a built-in support group and are a great place to start.

• If in doubt about what to do in a place, just *start walking* through your new environment. Walk until your day becomes interesting—even if this means wandering out of town and strolling the countryside. Eventually you'll see a scene or meet a person that makes your walk worthwhile. If you get "lost" in the process, just take a bus or taxi to a local landmark and find your way back to your hotel from there.

• Keep a journal from the outset of your travels, and discipline yourself to make a new entry every day. Feel free to be as brief or as rambling as you want. Keep track of stories, events, feelings, differences, and impressions. The result will be a remarkable record of your experiences and growth.

DAY-TO-DAY ERRANDS

• Because vagabonding involves taking your whole life on the road, some of your time each week will be devoted to basic errands, such as buying train tickets, doing laundry, changing money, shopping for toiletries, and sending e-mails. Allotting a certain time each week to take care of these matters will keep such tasks from continually interrupting your more interesting travel pursuits.

• When changing currency, always count your money before you leave the bank or exchange counter, just in case the teller makes a mistake. In countries where black-market exchange rates are preferable, try to make your transaction at a fixed business (hotels and jewelry stores are common for this) instead of a public space. Make sure you agree on a rate, count the dealer's cash before you hand over yours, and don't accept sailed or torn bills. In countries with weak currency, ask for large-denomination bills, as massive piles of small bills are hard to count. If at any point your black-marketeer begins to act suspicious (for instance, by making unusual requests or acting aggressive), exercise your right to walk away.

• Avoid the urge to make too many of your on-the-ground transportation arrangements at once, as this will stunt your spontaneity. Even multistop discount programs, such as the famous Eurail train pass, are only a bargain if you're constantly moving from place to place. Advance reservations are fine (and, in the case of trains, often necessary), but only for one trip at a time.

• Some places (such as India) have cheap and ubiquitous laundry services, but many don't. Fortunately, washing your own clothes is something you can easily do yourself. Bring a universal stopper for your hotel-room sink, and use shampoo as detergent. Bring a small bungee cord to use as a drying line. If your clothes are still a bit damp in the morning, the best solution is to wear them that day (which, while uncomfortable at first, beats having damp clothes inside your pack).

• Most people in the world don't subsist on supermarket-style canned goods, microwaved meals, and packaged snacks. Brave the open-air food markets—and be healthier for the experience!

ACCOMMODATIONS AND FACILITIES

• Finding hotels and guesthouses as you travel is rarely a problem, so don't bother with reservations. The only exceptions would be 1) when local festivals or tourist high season threaten to make hotel rooms scarce, and 2) if your incoming flight arrives late and you want to avoid the hassle of searching out a hotel room in the middle of the night.

- In most places, cheap hotels and guesthouses are locally owned, which means that budget travel is actually the best way to support the local economy. Moreover, locally owned accommodations are usually open to bargaining for room rates—especially during tourist low season. Many places offer a discounted rate for a multi-night stay.

- Never check into a room without asking to see it first. Check that the electricity and water work properly, and make sure the door locks are functional. Note the location of your room in relation to discos, mosques, factories, major streets, or other surroundings that might prove noisy at certain times of the day or night.

- When you leave your room for a day of adventure, take a hotel business card with you—just in case you get disoriented and forget where you're staying (which, believe it or not, is a surprisingly common travel occurrence). Even if you can't find your way back to the address on the card, a taxi driver can.

- Hole-in-the-floor "squatty-potty" toilets are the rule rather than the exception in many parts of the world. If you plan on traveling outside the standard tourist routes, you'd best learn how to use them. Fortunately, squatty-potties are very sanitary—though you'll want to pack your own toilet paper if you'd prefer not to "wipe" with water.

- Now that Internet cafés can be found nearly everywhere, receiving messages from home is rarely a problem. Should you want to receive a *package* from home, however, you'll want to take advantage of the *poste restante* system, whereby post offices worldwide will hold incoming mail for about a month. To avoid having your package misplaced, have the sender capitalize and underline your family name in large block letters, and send it to the general post office (GPO) of your destination city. If you're not sure where the GPO is, check your guidebook or ask a hotel clerk. The following template works best for addressing *poste restante* packages:

> <u>LAST NAME,</u> First name
> Poste Restante
> GPO
> City
> COUNTRY

BARGAINING

Outside of the industrialized world, fixed prices are used primarily in restaurants and on buses. Nearly every other product and service on the planet (from hotels to souvenirs to market goods) is open to negotiation—and only a fool would accept an opening price without haggling a little. Below are a few tips for braving the world of nonfixed prices.

Souvenirs

- Despite the exotic wonders that abound once you arrive overseas, avoid the compulsion to immediately start buying souvenirs. Not only will this save you the trouble of carrying these treasures around with you for the rest of your trip, but you'll also have a better feel for how and what to buy after you've traveled around for a while.

- When bargaining, let the merchant make the first offer—and don't respond by offering half the price and haggling from there. The merchants already expect you to do this, and they adjust their prices accordingly. Instead, see if the merchant will make another, lower offer before you start making bids. As you haggle, remain friendly and assertive (even playful), and try not to be rude or condescending. Conversely, don't let the merchant sway you with emotional pleas and melodramatics. Remember that he or she is much more experienced at this than you, and one of the most successful sales techniques in markets worldwide is to make First World shoppers feel *guilty* for not spending more money on something.

- Rule No. 1 as a conscientious shopper: Never offer a price on an item and then refuse to pay it. If you're not sure you want something, don't make a bid on it, period.

- In most tourist areas, souvenir shops sell similar items. Make comparisons before you make your purchase— and don't let merchants convince you that this is somehow impolite. Competition, after all, is how healthy markets thrive.

- Bargaining can be very difficult during tourist high season, when vacationers are happy to pay inflated prices for just about anything. If possible, save your souvenir shopping for low season; the products are the same, but the merchants will more likely be in a position to compromise.

Taxis and Transportation

- Taxi meters can be a confusing issue overseas. Some taxis will have them, and others won't. Some taxi meters will be "broken," while others will be outdated. Thus, don't assume all taxis are the same. Make sure that the meter works before you agree to a ride, and make sure the driver turns it on.

- Taxis without meters are common and legitimate worldwide. Just make sure you agree on a price *before* you go. Don't get into the taxi until the price is settled, and avoid drivers who try to hurry or bully you into the cab before a price is quoted.

- Avoid putting your bags into the trunk of a taxi, as this is often used as a bargaining chip by dodgy taxi drivers. If you have no choice but to use the trunk, make sure to remove all your baggage from the trunk before you pay your driver.

- In some places (such as China), taxi and bus drivers will quote you a certain fare in advance, then try to charge you double by claiming that your baggage "counts as one passenger." Unless your bag is obviously occupying its own bus seat, this is not a legitimate demand. Thus, clarify in advance that the price you're paying is for yourself as well as your luggage.

- Similarly, some taxi drivers will quote a price for your group, then claim it was a *per person* price when it comes time to pay up. This is obviously a scam, and the best way to avoid it is to clarify in advance whether the price applies to individuals or the whole group.

- For the most part, taxi and bus drivers are interesting, friendly people with great stories to tell. Be on your guard for the occasional scammer, but don't be reflexively paranoid or discourteous with your driver. After all, your road safety is in his hands!

VAGABONDING VOICES

I go to places within a country for the most ridiculous reasons—it may just have an interesting name or be close to a mountain with an interesting name, or I may pass through an area usually missed, maybe on some traveling "errand," but just decide to check it out and see what adventures I can make happen there. Travel is like a giant blank canvas, and the painting on the canvas is only limited by one's imagination.

—ROSS MORLEY, 25,
ENTREPRENEUR, ENGLAND

———

Keep your eyes open, experience more and "see" less. The "sights" have a tendency to merge together. How many Gothic cathedrals can you really appreciate?

—DAN NEELY, 26,
RAFT GUIDE, ARIZONA

Plenty of times I don't really seek . . . things just come to me. Even when I want to be "left alone," it doesn't seem to happen. However, I have the good fortune of meeting the kindest people wherever I go, so it's usually a huge bonus. I generally will hit big touristy things that interest me (Wat Pho, Durbar Square, Taj Mahal, etc.) and stay away from touristy areas that don't. I go with the flow and go with how I feel. I try not to set high goals and expectations.

—SERENA M. COLLINS, 27,
TEACHER AND GRADUATE
STUDENT, NEW YORK

John Muir

Only by going alone in silence, without baggage, can one truly get into the heart of the wilderness. All other travel is mere dust and hotels and baggage and chatter.

—JOHN MUIR, 1888 LETTER TO HIS WIFE

Widely regarded as America's first true environmentalist, John Muir exemplified how travel is best approached with a vivid and passionate interest in one's surroundings.

Born in Scotland in 1838 and raised in Wisconsin, Muir briefly lost his eyesight in a shop accident at age twenty-nine. When he regained his vision, a month later, he resolved to strike out and see the fabulous sights—forests, mountains, lakes—that he'd nearly been denied. Setting off on foot, he walked one thousand miles, from Indianapolis to the Gulf of Mexico. Eventually, he made his way to California, where he fell in love with Yosemite and the Sierra Nevada. Ultimately, his peripatetic life took him to places as far as Alaska, South America, Australia, Africa, Japan, and China.

From the beginning, Muir's travels were fueled by a passion for nature, and he always absorbed himself in studying the flora and geology of the places he visited. He was never in a hurry to reach his destination, and he once told a friend that "a delay of forty years or more" didn't bother him as long as he could explore other wildernesses along the way.

Muir believed that the worst mistake you can make in life is to consider yourself separate from your destinations, experiences, and surroundings. "As soon as we take one thing by itself," he wrote, "we find it hitched to everything in the universe."

CHAPTER 6

Travel is the best way we have of rescuing the humanity of places, and saving them from abstraction and ideology.

—PICO IYER, "WHY WE TRAVEL"

Meet Your Neighbors

In India, there's an old parable about a wise king who sent two of his court officers away to explore faraway lands. One of the courtiers, the king had observed, was arrogant and self-absorbed; the other was generous and open-minded. After many months of travel and exploration, both men returned home to report their findings. When the king questioned the men about the cities they visited, the generous courtier said that he found the people of foreign lands to be hospitable, generally kindhearted, and not much different from the people one met at home. On hearing this, the arrogant officer scoffed with envy, because the cities he'd visited were full of scheming liars, cheats, and wicked barbarians. Listening to these reports, the king laughed to himself—for he had sent both men to the same places.

"We see as we are," said the Buddha, and rarely is this quite so evident as when we travel. Unlike a simple vacation (where you rarely have time to interact with your environment), vagabonding revolves around the people you meet on the road—and the attitude you take into these encounters can make or break your entire travel experience. "If you view the world as a predominately hostile place, it will be," wrote Ed Buryn. By this same logic, of course, a positive worldview can lead to inspiring, human-centered road experiences.

Some of the people you'll meet while vagabonding will be fellow wanderers, many of them hailing from North America, Europe, Australia, or Japan. Because these other travelers naturally share your interests, values, and freedom, they are some of the most engaging and trustworthy people you'll meet on the road. At times—while hiking up some misty mountain with travel pals, or drunkenly philosophizing while waiting for a beachfront sunrise—you'll wonder how you were ever so lucky to meet such cool, laid-back, open-minded people. Many of these fellow vagabonders will become your long-distance friends (and, on occasion, your long-distance lovers) for months and years to come. Moreover, it's amazing the things you can learn about the home cultures of your various travel buddies. Over the years, I've sung Norwegian drinking songs in Burma, learned the intricacies of Chilean politics in Latvia, and been tutored in the art of Japanese table manners in Jordan. Traveling with Canadians has taught me more about Canada than I ever learned in my various weekend visits to Vancouver, and my countless conversations with Brits have led me to realize just how confused two people can become while supposedly speaking the same language.

Of course, you should never get too cliquish about hanging out with other travelers. "If you greet only your brothers," Jesus taught, "what are you doing more than others?" Indeed, in leaving home, you'll find that the most intriguing experiences and eye-opening encounters come from people whose lifestyles and backgrounds are completely different than your own. Which encounter, after all, will teach you the most in Punjab: drinking Kingfisher lager with friendly agnostic New Zealanders or sipping tea with friendly Indian Sikhs? Which activity would you enjoy most in Cuba: scuba diving with a gregarious German college student or rumba dancing with a gregarious Havana grandmother? Which of these experiences would you most likely share with your friends when you got home? Which would you remember best in your old age?

> Those who visit foreign nations, but associate only with their own countrymen, change their climate, but not their customs. They see new meridians, but the same men; and with heads as empty as their pockets, return home with traveled bodies, but untraveled minds.
>
> —CHARLES CALEB COLTON, *LACON*

Much of what's memorable in meeting people from faraway lands is how these interactions wind up teaching you about your own, culture-fed instincts. What is right and wrong in America doesn't always apply in other countries—and if you continually view other people through your own values, you'll lose the opportunity to see the world through *their* eyes. Americans, for example, value individualism, whereas most Asian cultures see individualism as a selfish betrayal of duty and family. Westerners prefer to be direct and objective in business dealings, whereas many Easterners see this as cold and dehumanized. People in some cultures will judge you on the basis of your religion (or lack thereof). Others will react strangely to your affluence (or lack of it), appearance, or gender. To read about such cultural differences is one thing, but to *experience* them is quite another. After all, cultural identity is *instinctive,* not intellectual—and this means that the challenge will come not in how you manage your own manners but in how you instinctively *react* to the unfamiliar manners of others.

When I was teaching English in Korea, for example, I became frustrated by my students' reaction to my informal teaching style. Thinking that my college-aged pupils would be more inspired to practice their English if they regarded me as a friend instead of a teacher, I conducted many of my "classes" in coffee shops and pubs. My students seemed to enjoy this unusual study environment, but they always clammed up when I referred to them as my "friends." "We are *not* your friends," one studious sophomore insisted. "We will *never be* your friends." Her response, which I initially took as hostility toward me as a non-Korean, left me feeling depressed. It wasn't until months later that I finally came to understand how the Korean notion of friendship is vastly different than that of the West. By their Confucian system of manners,

> **We do not need to understand other people and their customs fully to interact with them and learn in the process; it is making the effort to interact without knowing all the rules, improvising certain situations, that allows us to grow.**
>
> **—MARY CATHERINE BATESON,**
> ***PERIPHERAL VISIONS***

"friendship" is reserved for people of similar social status—and to regard a teacher as a "friend" (rather than a superior) would be a grave insult for both parties.

In this way, cultural awareness is often the positive product of rather negative experiences—and no amount of sensitivity training can compare to what you'll learn by accident. After all, the very concept of "cultural sensitivity" is something we understand through the liberal, democratic, egalitarian taint of our own culture, and these very assumptions might actually be offensive to some ways of thinking. The point of travel, then, is not to evaluate the rightness or wrongness of other cultures (after all, you could stay at home to do that) but to better *understand* them.

Thus, the secret to interacting with people in foreign lands is not to fine-tune your sense of political correctness (which itself is a Western construct) but to fine-tune your sense of *humor*. Most comedy, after all, is simply a displacement of context—Jack Lemmon dressing up as a woman, Andy Kaufman lip-synching the *Mighty Mouse* theme song, Jerry Seinfeld dating a woman whose name he can't remember—and where can you find a more radical context displacement than in traveling to distant lands? The ability to laugh at yourself and take things in stride can thus be the key to enduring strange new cultural situations.

And while humor might seem like a fairly contemporary way to deal with unfamiliar environments, it's actually a time-honored travel strategy. Fourteenth-century Moroccan vagabonder Ibn Battuta frequently exercised his self-effacing sense of humor during a twenty-eight-year journey through Africa, Asia, and the Middle East. In one instance that reminds me of my own travel experiences, Battuta found himself lost in a Persian city and asked a local dervish if he could speak

Arabic. *"Na'am,"* the dervish replied, using the courteous Arabic word for yes. Encouraged, Battuta then proceeded to ask at great length about the nearest hospice—only to discover that *na'am* was the only word of Arabic the dervish knew. (Similarly, I once spent two hours wandering the Philippine port of Cebu before realizing that yes-or-no questions would never help me locate an ATM machine.)

The most vivid bit of cultural displacement from Battuta's *Travels*, however, comes when the peripatetic Moroccan visits "the infidel sultan of Mul-Jawa" in Indonesia:

> *While this sultan was sitting in audience, I saw a man with a knife in his hand resembling a bookbinder's tool. He put the knife to his own neck, and delivered a long speech which I did not understand, then gripped it with both hands and cut his own throat. So sharp was the knife and so strong his grip that his head fell to the ground. I was amazed at his action.*
>
> *The sultan turned to me and said, "Does anyone do this in your country?"*

If Battuta could wing his way through this situation, you should be able to handle the comparatively benign encounters that come your way while vagabonding.

On the road, a big prerequisite for keeping your sense of humor is to first cultivate a sense of humility. After all, it can be hard to laugh at yourself if you swagger through the world like you own it.

Only a few centuries ago, humility was not even an option for travelers; it was a survival necessity. Medieval explorers groveled in deference to petty regional governors as reflexively as modern travelers apply for visas, and even Marco Polo was forced to do his share of cowering before the Great Khan. (Indeed, if you think arrogant bureaucrats test your pride and patience at international borders, just keep in mind visitors to the sixteenth-century East African court of Karanga, who were forced to approach the local monarch by rhythmically clapping their hands as they slithered on their stomachs through fresh cow dung.) This in mind, it's amazing the degree of diplomatic immunity that modern travel affords you. Even in isolated areas, where the formal laws that guarantee your safety and self-esteem are a mere abstraction, people for the most part treat travelers with warmth and hospitality.

The art of learning fundamental common values is perhaps the greatest gain of travel to those who wish to live at ease among their fellows.

—FREYA STARK, *PERSEUS IN THE WIND*

Diplomatic immunity notwithstanding, humility is always a useful lifestyle accessory when encountering new cultures. In *The Wisdom of the Desert,* Thomas Merton recalls the story of a fourth-century monk who was ordered by his abbot to give money to whoever insulted him. After faithfully doing this for three years, the monk was then instructed to travel to Athens to further his studies. Merton reports:

> *The disciple was entering Athens when he met a certain man who sat at the gate insulting everybody who came and went. He also insulted the disciple, who immediately burst out laughing.*
>
> *"Why do you laugh when I insult you?" said the man.*

"Because," said the disciple, "for three years I have been paying for this kind of thing and now you give it to me for nothing."

"Enter the city," said the man, "it is all yours."

On the vagabonding road, it's not even likely you'll get insulted all that often, but this whimsical analogy still applies. After all, if you can find joy in insults—if you can learn to laugh at what would otherwise have made you angry—the world is indeed "all yours" as a cross-cultural traveler.

If there's a danger in cultural openness and humility, it's the ease with which you can get carried away with it. Sometimes, the simplicity, poverty, and purity of other cultures will seem so intriguing (indeed, so close to what you are trying to seek as a vagabonder) that you'll be tempted to completely ditch your own culture in favor of exotic new ideals. Known in the nineteenth century as "romantic primitivism," this naive compulsion to buy wholesale into the perceived virtues of other cultures climaxed with the celebrated exodus of Western hippies to India in the late 1960s. Two decades later, Indian writer Gita Mehta scathingly suggested that these hippie seekers were little more than confused buffoons who mistook "orgies of self-indulgence" for revealed mysticism.

"What an entrance," wrote Mehta in *Karma Cola*. "Thousands and thousands of them, clashing cymbals, ringing bells, playing flutes, wearing bright colors and weird clothes, singing, dancing and speaking in tongues . . . [a] caravanserai of libertine celebrants who were wiping away the proprieties of caste, race, and sex by sheer stoned incomprehension. The seduction lay in the chaos. They thought we were simple. We thought they were neon. They thought we were profound. We knew we were provincial. Everyone thought everybody else was ridiculously exotic and everybody got it wrong."

Tourist scholars have attributed such half-baked cultural obsession to the ever-changing (and somewhat alienating) face of modern society itself. In seeking to become a part of these more traditional cultures, scholars say, modern travelers are trying to validate their sense of authenticity and rediscover their own lost connections to the past. This isn't just a hippie cliché, either. An entire industry of "ethno-tourism" has now grown up around this sentimental fascination with isolated societies. In the Amazon, guided tourists spend days in the jungle seeking to interact with Stone Age tribes. In Greenland, tour clients pay top dollar to go on traditional Inuit seal hunts. In the South Pacific, nearly forgotten dance traditions have been revived solely to entertain vacationers.

> Persons who propose to themselves a scheme for traveling generally do it with a view to rub off local prejudices . . . and to acquire that enlarged and impartial view of men and things which no single country can afford.
>
> —JOSIAH TUCKER, "INSTRUCTIONS FOR TRAVELLERS"

This tourist fascination with the exotic has yielded mixed results. As isolated cultures come into closer contact with modern visitors, they naturally become more and more likely to seek modern conveniences for themselves. The more these ethnic enclaves accumulate radios and motorbikes, of course, the less "authentic" they seem to appear—and thus they become less appealing to tourists. In places like Bali, ethnic villages have resorted to "staged authenticity" (hiding televisions and swapping T-shirts for ethnic outfits when tour buses show up) just to maintain their tourism-dependent economy. Granted,

Balinese villagers are just as Balinese when dressed in blue jeans, but that simply doesn't jibe with the fickle market demands of ethno-tourism. Consequently, we end up with these surreal scenarios, wherein tourists from Los Angeles will travel to Thailand to see relatively modernized Hmong villagers don ethnic costumes, yet those same tourists would never think to visit a community of similarly modern Hmong-Americans in Los Angeles. As historian Dagobert Runes quipped, "People travel to faraway places to watch, in fascination, the kind of people they ignore at home."

Or, to paraphrase a joke from *Seinfeld,* many ethno-tourists aren't traveling the world to interact with exotic people—they're traveling the world to interact with exotic *clothing.*

To truly interact with people as you travel, then, you have to learn to see other cultures not as *National Geographic* snapshots but as *neighbors.* And, as with neighbors in your hometown, interaction with people in faraway lands is a two-way street. Indeed, as exotic as the Siberian Chukchi or the Namibian Bushmen seem to you, there's a good chance you'll seem exotic to them as well. "The simplest fact of our neighbors' lives may read like a fairy tale to us," wrote Pico Iyer in *The Global Soul.* "The forgotten, tonic appendix to that is that our lives, in their tiniest details, may seem marvelous to them, and one virtue of [traveling] in so strange a place is to be reminded daily of how strange I seem to it."

This mutual fascination will serve to enrich your en-

Leaving home is a kind of forgiveness, and when you get among strangers, you're amazed at how decent they seem. Nobody smirks at you or gossips about you, nobody resents your successes or relishes your defeats. You get to start over, a sort of redemption.

—GARRISON KEILLOR, *LEAVING HOME*

counters on the road, since it allows you to learn (as well as teach) about your *own* home as you begin to meet your global neighbors.

Cross-Cultural Interactions Q & A

How do I go about meeting locals in my travels?

In your day-to-day vagabonding experience, meeting locals will rarely prove a problem. From touts at the airport to sheepherders on remote mountains, you will rarely find yourself alone as you travel. It is important to remember, however, that the nature of your relationship to these "neighbors" will not be the same in every situation.

Your gender, for example, will affect how people react to you. Indeed, while most everything I say in this book applies equally to men and women, cross-cultural social interactions are a major exception. This is because women travelers more frequently tend to be the target of curiosity, harassment, and double standards. Simple friendliness and eye contact can be taken the wrong way by men in traditional cultures, and female independence is strangely confused with sexual lasciviousness in many parts of the world. It's not fair, but it's a reality—so female travelers should be on their guard. Most good guidebooks will contain culture-specific advice for female travelers, often pertaining to conservative dress codes. And while it might not be enjoyable to wear a chador in a place like Iran (especially when male travelers can wear normal Western clothes), the experience can provide you with unique insights into the lives of women in that part of the world. Moreover, being female often has its social advantages in conservative cultures. I enjoyed my five-month sojourn through the Middle East, for example, but the separation of the sexes within Muslim countries never allowed me to know how Arab women live and think. I found myself in envy of female travelers, who (despite occasional harassment at the hands of local Casanovas) were able to have meaningful encounters with men and women alike.

Apart from gender, the nature of your relationship to the locals will also depend on *where* in a culture you are traveling. At the risk of sounding ridiculously reductive, I'll point out two primary social arenas for travelers to any culture: tourist areas and nontourist areas. Both provide good opportunities for genuine human interaction, but it's important to be able to distinguish between the two, because people tend to view you differently in each. Basic cultural codes of manners, of course, apply to both areas. (And again, any good guidebook will have culture-specific information on local manners, including such simple issues as body language, dress codes, tipping, and table etiquette.)

What are "tourist areas," and how do they affect my relationship to the locals?

Regardless of whether or not you consider yourself a "tourist" (as opposed to a "traveler"—a silly distinction that I'll address later), there's no avoiding the fact that you'll spend much of your travel time in tourist areas, which include airports, hotels, bus and train stations, major city centers, historical sites, nature parks, national monuments, and anyplace travelers congregate in large numbers.

In these tourist areas many locals will use friendship as a front to tout hotels or sell souvenirs. As annoying as this can be, this strategy is not necessarily a calculating capitalistic scam. After all, the formal tourist industry developed out of traditional hospitality, and many locals will take a genuine interest in you even as they try to sell you things. In this way, many of your initial interactions on the road will be with locals who are offering a service—cabdrivers, guesthouse clerks, shopkeepers. Many of these folks will like you mainly for your money (and indeed, your money is what feeds their families), but some of them have plenty to offer as genuine friends and cultural hosts. Of all the locals I hung out with in Egypt, my truest Egyptian friend was a hotel clerk who accompanied me to movies and markets during his time off from work. Of all the people I met in Burma, I learned the most about the local culture from a trishaw driver who (after pedaling me around on a paid tour of the Sagaing area) took me home to meet his family and insisted I sleep for free at the neighborhood monastery.

Of course, by the virtue of sheer tourist numbers, not every hotel clerk and trishaw driver will be interested in sincere friendship. "Tourism can be a bridge to an appreciation of cultural relativity and international understanding," wrote Valene L. Smith in *Hosts and Guests: The Anthropology of Tourism.* "However, catering to guests is a repetitive, monotonous business, and although questions posed by each visitor may be 'new' to him, hosts can become as bored as if a cassette has been turned on." Beyond this, you can't even assume that interactions are always better than transactions when dealing with people in foreign lands. Surveys in Australia have revealed that Aborigines actually prefer the impersonal dealings of mass tourists to sincere wanderers, since bus loads of package-guided guests are more likely to buy souvenirs and less likely to ask a lot of annoying questions. "We certainly can appreciate the motives and goodwill of adventuresome tourists who want to become more closely involved with the people they visit," observed tourism scholar Erve Chambers. "But it can be disarming to discover that some tourist hosts might be more content to just have the tourists' money—and be rid of them."

Even when your interaction with locals is clearly impersonal and transaction-based, be sure to abide by the rules of simple courtesy. Exercise your smiling muscles, practice your charm, and try to let go of your own cultural assumptions in regard to how people should treat you. Most cultures, after all, aren't familiar with the rigorous American standards of customer service, and few people in the world make a fetish of personal "rights" quite the way we do in the industrialized West. Put yourself in a local person's shoes before you judge him for his actions, and don't lose your cool over a misunderstood restaurant order or a late bus. Even when dealing with pushy vendors and aggressive touts, a firm, courteous "no thanks" is always better than an angry rebuff. Make an effort to never lose your temper within other cultures—regardless of how tired and frustrated you are—as this will only make your situation worse. Try not to bully or manipulate your way into getting what you want (and, of course, don't let touts or vendors bully, manipulate, or "guilt" you into buying something *you* don't want). If worse comes to worst, simply ignore whoever's bothering you.

A lot of the confusion and discord that can arise between travelers and locals revolves around money. Thus, while it's important to practice thrift on the vagabonding road, it's equally important *not* to be obsessive about your budget. It's one thing to spend money conscientiously but another to tenaciously scrap for the lowest possible price in countries where the average annual domestic income is smaller than what you'd pay to fly home. Indeed, few things are more ridiculous than the spectacle of a "budget traveler" losing his temper at a rickshaw driver over ten cents while negotiating a ride to a bar where he'll blow ten dollars on beer. Be aware that you occupy an economic dynamic wherever you go—and that there is no particular virtue in compulsively avoiding expenses (especially when many of those expenses are of direct benefit to local families). On one hand, it's good to be aware of the going rate for local products and services, since (while the prices may seem cheap compared to home) continually overpaying will only confuse the vendor and jack up the price for other travelers who come along. On the other hand, it's hard to sympathize with a First World traveler who squeezes another month out of a Third World country by sleeping in the forest and hitching rides. (Better to spend that month back home sacking groceries and saving up for a trip that benefits local bus drivers and hotel maids.)

If there's a rule of thumb for conscientiously spending money on the road, it's to watch what the locals do. Not only will this make you better aware of local prices and procedures, it will give you cultural pointers on everything from haggling for bargains to dealing with beggars. And, even if you do occasionally get "ripped off" as an outsider, remember that even this is part of a time-honored tradition. After all, cross-cultural commerce is one of the oldest forms of peaceful exchange on the planet, and getting gouged three extra dollars for that souvenir demon mask (as I was once in Mongolia) is certainly preferable to certain historical alternatives, like getting hacked to pieces at the town gate.

What about interactions in nontourist areas?

Away from tourist zones, the most awkward aspect of visiting some places won't be the natives' interest in your money but their interest in *you*. In areas that don't see many outsiders, your presence will literally stop activity in the streets. Children will squeal and point. Teens will yell "hello" in ridiculous, singsong voices. Adults will stare in wonder at your foreign skin, hair, height, or clothing. When you stop to rest or eat, crowds will gather to watch your actions in seeming fascination. At times, you'll be amazed—and exhausted—by people's capacity to take intense interest in you for hours on end. Once, while traveling through the northwestern frontier of Cambodia, I enjoyed four days of such celebrity status in a village called Opasat. One elderly villager was so intrigued upon meeting me that she yanked off my size 13 sandals and started pulling on my toes. At first I thought this was some sort of massage technique, until she reached into my shirt and started tugging at my nipple hair.

Of course, not every encounter outside of tourist areas will involve anthropological curiosity at the hands of isolated villagers. Some of the people who take an interest in you will be urban, middle-class locals who are simply curious to hear your views about sports, politics, or pop culture. And while natives who wear American fashions and drop hip-hop slang into their conversations might not live up to your exotic travel fantasies, remember that they, too, are a genuine part of your host culture. Despite globalization-fueled fears, Air Jordans and Internet access have not turned the middle classes of the world into robotic American clones—and your workaday Lima business accountant can give you a glimpse of Peru that is just as authentic as what his potato-farming Andean countrymen can offer. Indeed, some of your most interesting encounters on the road will come from natives who share the same profession as you. Regardless of whether you're a student, a Web designer, or a truck driver, it's always fascinating (and educational) to strike up a friendship with a local who shares your calling. As a former teacher, I found that some of my best road experiences in places like Hungary, Lebanon, and the Philippines came when local educators asked me to participate in their English classes.

You'll be amazed by how often you can meet locals merely by strolling around with a smile, but this isn't always a sure method of interacting with people in new environments. At times, locals will be a bit shy or distracted, so it's good to know how to engage them. One simple option is to approach local folks and ask them where you can find a good restaurant. Even if they can't understand you, most people will take an interest and try to help (or, in many cases, they'll send for the neighborhood's star English speaker—usually a teenage student or a well-traveled elder). Public gathering places, such as cafés, bars, and tea shops, are always good sites to mix and interact with locals, since caffeine and alcohol always inspire people to conversation and extroversion. Sports and music are also great ways to meet people, should you be willing to share your musical or athletic skills (or lack thereof) on street corners and makeshift playing fields. I've lost countless volleyball matches this way in Thailand—but won plenty of friends.

Many people use a camera to break the ice in public situations—though you should always ask permission before taking someone's photo (and never renege on a promise to send someone a copy!). Conversely, be sure to carry photos of yourself, your hometown, and your family to show to people on the road. Not only do such pictures make good conversation pieces (or keepsakes, should you have several copies), they can humanize you to people who might otherwise consider you somewhat of a curiosity. Once, while taking a share-taxi through Egypt's Western Desert, I found myself sitting next to a pious Muslim gentleman who proceeded to scold me at length about "decadent" American values. When my verbal defense of American life proved futile, I changed the subject by breaking out photos of my parents, my grandfather, and my baby nephews. Before long, the man was asking me all kinds of earnest and downright friendly questions about life in the United States. Whereas before I'd been just another sunburned infidel in hiking shorts, my pictures created a common ground by showing that I cared for my family just as he cared for his.

One final foolproof method of interacting with people on the road is to play with the local children. Unlike adults, kids won't be intimidated by language barriers, and they will be happy to giggle at your silly faces, join you in spontaneous games, and sing along to simple tunes. (In dealing with children, however, keep in mind that the best gift you can give them is your time and energy. Some travelers give sweets or pens to kids, thinking perhaps to show goodwill or encourage literacy, but—to the contrary—this usually just encourages kids to beg sweets and pens from the next travelers who come along.)

How do I bridge the "language gap" while traveling?

One big advantage of twenty-first-century travel is that English has become the lingua franca for much of the world. Even if you don't always find fluent speakers, you can usually find locals (often students) who know a few phrases of English. When speaking English to nonfluent listeners, remember that loudness is not what will make you understood. Rather, you should make an effort to speak *slowly, simply,* and *clearly.* And, when *listening* to nonfluent English, be patient and try to figure out mispronounced words from the context of what is being said. Keep in mind that many people know English only from study dictionaries—not spoken and heard conversation—and thus might not know how to sound words correctly. Try to develop an ear for imperfect "Tarzan English," and keep in mind that it's probably much clearer than your "Tarzan" rendering of the local tongue. Compliment anyone brave (and helpful) enough to try his or her English on you, and try to develop a knack for cross-cultural small talk (which involves simple topics that everyone can relate to, such as family, food, hobbies, and love life or marital status).

Pocket language guides can also be good for cross-cultural communication; at times you can have entire (albeit slow) conversations just by flipping through the pages of your phrasebook. And regardless of your adeptness at picking up new languages, it's never too hard to commit a few words and phrases of the local language to memory. Lazy afternoons and long bus rides provide good opportunities to begin your memorization. Useful starting phrases include *hello; please* and *thank you; yes* and *no;* the numbers one to ten, plus one hundred and one thousand; *How much?; Where is it?;* and *No problem!* Additional useful words to learn are those for *hotel, bus station, restaurant, toilet, good, bad,* and *beer.* Any local idioms and slang you can pick up will delight the locals (so long as you aren't learning something profane or offensive). And, of course, improvised sign language and face pulling can go a long way toward getting your point across. Regardless of whether you try verbal or visual communication, your efforts will invariably provoke lots of laughter—so be ready to laugh along!

How do I respond to offers of hospitality?

In a tourist zone, such invitations should make you wary of a scam (or, at the very least, a tedious trip to the souvenir shop of your host's "uncle"). Similarly, females traveling solo in conservative cultures should regard hospitality offers with extreme caution.

In most other settings, however, hospitality is a basic form of human-to-human communion—and it's always rewarding to share a meal or spend the night with local hosts. Interestingly, I've found that most such invitations come from individuals or families that have a comparatively low standard of living. Since hosting a relatively "wealthy" guest will be a matter of pride for these folks, don't insult them with an ostentatious, guilt-ridden refusal, or a magnanimous offer to foot the bill. Instead, take them up on their offer, but bring along a simple gift (either something from the local market or bottle shop or small souvenirs from home). If you'd like to share your gifts with the children, ask the parents' permission first. Be sensitive and respectful to your hosts and their culture, and don't be averse to taking a polite sip of arak or goat stew, even if you normally consider yourself a teetotaler or vegetarian. And, of course, don't exploit the institution of hospitality; it can be disheartening to see travelers manipulating local generosity, or taking it for granted.

As a vagabonder and a cultural guest, learn to pay back what you've received by spotting need and practicing generosity elsewhere (even with other travelers) as you travel from place to place. The Hungarians who picked me up hitchhiking in eastern Europe never let me chip in for gas, for instance, but their generosity inspired me to give twenty dollars to a Japanese backpacker who'd lost his money belt in Vienna. Odds are, that Japanese traveler was encouraged to pass on the goodwill elsewhere. Thus, even in an indirect way, try to give as much as you take when you travel—even if this means taking an attitude of generosity home with you.

What if I get tired of meeting so many people as I travel?

If you've had your fill of exotic company, take a break. Hang out with other travelers, or bury your nose in a book for a while. Meeting the locals can be rewarding, but that doesn't mean you have to compulsively seek friendships wherever you go. Let things happen. Keep your human interactions on a direct, person-to-person level, and don't "acquire" these experiences like souvenirs. Even if you find yourself in a positively extraordinary social situation (be it breakfast with Bollywood film stars, lunch with Congolese guerrillas, or dinner with Papuan headhunters), try to keep yourself in the moment instead of thinking about what kind of story it will make when you get home.

Such awareness will not only make you a better neighbor but will ensure that you'll never get homesick as you explore other places.

Tip Sheet

CULTURE SHOCK OVERSEAS

- Cultural awareness can be quite a challenge when traveling internationally. In some cultures, for example, it's polite to clean your plate during a dinner, whereas other cultures find it more courteous to leave a bit of food on your plate when you finish eating. Body language can also be confusing, as some cultures will consider you uncouth if you eat with your left hand, stand with your hands in your pockets, or beckon someone with your palm facing upward. A good guidebook will give culture-specific pointers for these kinds of issues (and some of the references below offer detailed advice).

• Most cultures are much more conservative than ours, and when you're a guest, it's good to respect these manner codes, even if you don't subscribe to them. Always maintain decorum in holy places, even if you aren't religious. And even if you find yourself in the midst of a passionate road romance, try to avoid public displays of affection.

• Don't be surprised if people in some cultures ask you seemingly intrusive questions. Topics such as age, income, and marital status are not particularly taboo in many parts of the world, so don't get offended if such subjects come up in conversation. Often, people will ask what you think of their country. Since some folks might be sensitive to your reply, the best response is not to opine but simply to ask questions about their culture. Most people will be flattered by your curiosity and happy to teach you about their homeland.

• If you strongly identify with your immigrant roots, a trip to your ethnic homeland could be the biggest culture shock of all. Regardless of whether your ancestors hailed from Africa, Asia, Europe, or Latin America, odds are your ethnic home will seem far more *foreign* than you'd expected. Many American-born travelers who make nostalgic pilgrimages "back" to places like Poland or Korea or Mexico usually get a vivid lesson in just how American they are.

CROSS-CULTURAL RESOURCES

Culture Shock! Guidebooks (Graphic Arts Publishing)
The books in this series provide a crash course in local customs and etiquette for dozens of individual countries around the world. Topics covered include political traditions, religious practices, monetary systems, body language, and making friends.

Do's and Taboos Around the World: A Guide to International Behavior, by Roger Axtell (John Wiley & Sons, 1993)
Advice for the business and pleasure traveler on what to do and what not to do in other cultures. Uses a blend of humor and curious facts to provide information on how to dress, deal with exotic food, pronounce names, exchange gifts, and interpret body language in nearly one hundred countries.

The Traveler's Guide to Latin American Customs and Manners, by Elizabeth Devin and Nancy L. Braganti (St. Martin's Press, 2000)
Pointers on how to converse, dine, tip, drive, bargain, dress, make friends, and conduct business in Latin America. This St. Martin's Press series also includes titles on African, Asian, European, and Middle Eastern customs and manners.

BootsnAll Toolkit: Phrasebooks (http://www.bootsnall
.com/tk/books/lingual.shtml)
This concise and well-organized Web guide links to thousands of phrasebooks and language guides for sale online. Organized by geographical region.

TravLang Travel and Language Services (www.travlang .com)
Online phrasebooks for numerous languages, as well as dictionaries for twenty-three languages available for download (to Palm or PC).

Cultural Survival Quarterly (www.cs.org)
A quarterly magazine covering the life and concerns of indigenous and minority cultures around the world; $45 for a one-year (four issues) subscription, which includes membership with the Harvard-affiliated organization of the same name.

FEMALE VAGABONDERS

It almost goes without saying that women travelers can go to the same places and do the same things on the road as their male counterparts. Not only is there a wide body of literature to prove this (see below), but a cursory visit to any travel scene in the world will reveal similar numbers of male and female vagabonders. Despite this seeming equality, however, women do have a few unique challenges to confront as they travel from place to place.

Safety

- Most foreign streets are as safe or safer than the streets at home. But, as with home, you must be wary of where you wander. Use your guidebook and word of mouth to know which areas to avoid, and never walk alone at night. Always be alert and aware of your surroundings, especially at night.

- Look and act confident, even when you aren't. Don't act lost (even when you are), and don't stand in the street with your map out, since potential criminals and hustlers will take this as an invitation to "help" you.

- When traveling alone, be cautious toward offers of hospitality, especially if the hospitality separates you from safe public areas. When in your hotel, make a habit of keeping your door locked at all times, and be suspicious if someone knocks on your door late at night.

- There's always safety in numbers. Even if you are a woman traveling solo, it's rarely difficult to find company in other travelers (male and female alike) should you feel the need.

Dealing with Men

- Most men in cultures around the world are honorable and respectful toward female travelers, but the few obnoxious exceptions will always stand out. Sooner or later, you *will* get harassed, so be ready to deflect the harassment with a no-nonsense attitude—and never let it get to you emotionally.

- The best way to avoid getting harassed in conservative cultures is to abide by the local dress code. Additionally, it never hurts to tone down your everyday courtesies on the road, since there are times when a friendly smile or a reflexive "Thank you" will give men the wrong idea. If a man makes an unwanted pass at you, shoot him down firmly and unambiguously. If he persists or becomes aggressive (and especially if he tries to grope you), a loud, angry "NO!" will shame him by drawing public attention to his actions. Often, you can get rid of

unwanted attention by mentioning that your big, strap-
ping boyfriend is due to return any minute. Even if no
such boyfriend exists, your harasser usually won't stick
around to meet him.

• Most traveler scenes (and beach hangouts in particular) have plenty of local Casanovas who are ready and
eager to sweep you off your feet with declarations of
love. If you're looking for a fling, fine. Just don't let yourself get charmed and flattered into an uncomfortable
situation. Tourist hustlers have their schemes down, so
hang on to your wallet as well as your heart.

Interacting with Local Women

• Never presume that you have more to teach local
women than they have to teach you. Feminist theory,
after all, is largely useless in conservative cultures, so
the best way to achieve solidarity with a local woman is
to listen to her and try to understand her worldview and
way of life.

• Sometimes you can alienate and distance yourself from
local women simply by being socially open and liber-
ated. Thus, make an effort to notice and emulate how
females dress and interact with men in your host culture. After all, a woman is far more likely to show you
hospitality if she can feel certain that you aren't some
foreign bimbo out to lure her men into temptation.

Resources for Female Travelers

*A Journey of One's Own: Uncommon Advice for the Inde-
pendent Woman Traveler,* by Thalia Zepatos (Eighth
Mountain Press, 1996)

Detailed advice on practical matters for women traveling alone overseas.

Gutsy Women: Travel Tips and Wisdom for the Road, by Marybeth Bond (Travelers' Tales, 1996)
A pocket guide with travel tips for women on the road, including travel vignettes and tips on things like safety and budgeting.

Safety and Security for Women Who Travel, by Sheila Swan and Peter Laufer (Travelers' Tales, 1998)
A collection of tips and wisdom to help female adventurers avoid trouble on the road and travel with security and confidence.

A Woman's World, edited by Marybeth Bond (Travelers' Tales, 1995)
An anthology of travel tales from more than fifty women travelers, including Gretel Ehrlich, Pam Houston, and Barbara Grizzuti Harrison.

Woman Travel: First-Hand Accounts from More Than Sixty Countries, edited by Natania Jansz, Miranda Davies, and Emma Drew (Rough Guides, 1999)
Inspiring travel tales written by women adventuring into all corners of the globe.

A Woman Alone: Travel Tales from Around the Globe, edited by Faith Conlon, Ingrid Emerick, and Christina Henry de Tessan (Seal Press, 2001)
A travel anthology featuring twenty-nine travel tales about women traveling alone.

Passionfruit: A Women's Travel Journal (http://passionfruit.com)

A magazine of travel tales and advice by and for women, with emphasis on independent and cross-cultural travel; $18 for a one-year (four issues) subscription. Some stories available online.

Journeywoman: The Premier Travel Resource for Women
(http://www.journeywoman.com)
Online articles, links, and travel advice for female travelers.

For a fully updated and linkable online version of this resource guide, surf to http://vagabonding.net/ and follow the "Resources" link.

VAGABONDING VOICES

The people you meet on the road are your window to the world. You can learn as much about the culture of a non-American travel companion as you can about the culture you're in. Think of your companions as a *National Geographic* special. You can never get tired of meeting people.

—DEAN BRAGONIER, 29,
BUSINESSMAN, MASSACHUSETTS

———

I meet local people and consider that an adventure. People are the interest. I once was invited into a Mayan home for three days in the mountains and was the guest of honor in the village and at church. No English or Spanish spoken— only Mayan Ixil. I learned that most people in this world just want the basics in life and to be happy with their people.

—DAN O'BRIEN, 62,
COMMERCIAL FISHERMAN, ALASKA

It's easy to put up barriers, reading books and e-mailing all the time, eating every meal at expat joints and drinking back at the hostel over a game of cards—and sometimes I need to get myself motivated to go out and do other stuff. Sure, expat cafés and card games have their place, but there's more to it than just that, and a lot of the other stuff involves just diving into the unknown—accepting an invitation to a wedding in some small town where you don't speak the language, or just wandering around the streets and alleys and talking to whomever strikes up a conversation with you, and so on. I kind of like spending a lot of time on my own, so it has been a challenge going out and doing stuff with local people.

—TOM BOURGUIGON, 25,
GRAPHIC DESIGNER, OHIO

———

The aphorism "The map is not the territory" looms ever larger as I get lost in the intricacies of a culture, giving up any hope of understanding, while love and appreciation between us grows.

—ELDON HAINES, 70,
NASA PLANETARY SCIENTIST,
OREGON

John Ledyard

He saw that if anyone appeared insane it was not the island cannibals or the grease-encrusted Aleuts or the stony-hearted Tartars, but the one who visited them. He saw that the true alien was the traveler.

—LARZER ZIFF, *RETURN PASSAGES*

Shortly before Lewis and Clark famously explored the American West, an equally intrepid American explored the world. His name was John Ledyard, and he was one of America's first—and most prolific—vagabonders.

Born in 1751, Ledyard attended college at Dartmouth, intending to be a missionary to the local Native Americans. Instead of proselytizing the natives, however, he ended up learning their backwoods skills—and at age twenty-three, he chopped down a pine tree, crafted it into a canoe, and paddled one hundred miles to the sea. He never looked back from there, as he went on to such adventures as sailing with Captain Cook's pioneering Pacific expedition and walking from Sweden to Siberia. In his travels, Ledyard made it a point to mingle with native cultures, not so he could romanticize them, but so he could understand how they perceived reality.

In *Return Passages*, critic Larzer Ziff describes a special quality of social tolerance and endurance in Ledyard—a trait that all vagabonders might do well to emulate: "He seemed the perfect democrat, at ease with those who were regarded as his betters, yet free of presumption, self-assured and not self-important; possessed of an urbanity acquired more from contact with the gentlemen of the primitive world than those of the city, and, most importantly, able to accept rebuffs—to *undergo* in order to go."

CHAPTER 7

We need sometimes to escape into open solitudes, into aimlessness, into the moral holiday of running some pure hazard, in order to sharpen the edge of life, to taste hardship, and to be compelled to work desperately for a moment no matter what.

—GEORGE SANTAYANA, "THE PHILOSOPHY OF TRAVEL"

Get into Adventures

A few hundred years ago, "adventure travel" involved brave expeditions into the terra incognita—the mysterious lands at the edge of the known world, thought to be populated by monsters and mermaids. The more these unknown areas were explored, the smaller the terra incognita became, and gradually the physical limits of the world ceased to be such a mythical secret. By the time Captain Cook's eighteenth-century explorations proved that no great continent existed in the South Pacific, it was no longer possible to "sail off the map"—and people have had trouble defining what "adventure" is ever since. As a result, the "final act" of adventure has been declared with each new global discovery or development over the last two centuries, from the exploration of inner Africa to Hillary and Norgay's ascent of Everest.

In recent years, the very notion of adventure travel has sometimes been written off as a self-deluded farce. In 2001, when millionaire Dennis Tito paid $20 million to travel into space with Russian cosmonauts, pundits groaned in disdain. "A tourist in space illustrates an age in which there are very few places left where adventure travel *can't* be found," wrote *Boston Globe* editor H. D. S. Greenway. "No remote village in the Himalayas or jungle clearing in Borneo is beyond tourism's reach."

The implication here is that adventure is still considered a purely *physical* act—a ritual of putting rugged distance between oneself and one's home. Without the lure of a terra incognita to guide us, such thinking goes, the legacy of adventure travel has been passed on to those who scale cliffs, dive wrecks, and hike jungles. In America especially (where no experience seems worthy of public mention unless it can be measured, competed, or broadcast before a television audience) modern adventure is associated with extreme sports, like ice climbing, street luge, or high-altitude endurance racing.

> Exploration is not so much a covering of surface distance as a study in depth: a fleeting episode, a fragment of landscape or a remark overheard that may provide the only means of understanding and interpreting areas which would otherwise remain barren of meaning.
>
> —CLAUDE LÉVI-STRAUSS,
> *TRISTES TROPIQUES*

This is all good fun, but any salty vagabonder can tell you that true adventure is not an experience that can be captured on television or sold like a commodity. Indeed, tour companies may have standardized "adventure travel" into set categories—rafting, mountaineering, skydiving, and so on—but this doesn't mean you have to buy into it (literally or figuratively). There's nothing inherently *wrong* with extreme sports and organized expeditions, of course, but real adventure is not something that can be itemized in glossy brochures or sports magazines. In fact, having an adventure is sometimes just a matter of going out and allowing things to happen in a strange and amazing new environment—not so much a physical challenge as a *psychic* one.

Which experience, for example, will require more innovation and persistence: buying into a guided expedition up some Andean peak (where you can eat freeze-dried turkey tetrazzini along the way and call your family via satellite phone from the summit) or lingering for a few weeks in some Bolivian village to learn a local craft without fully knowing the local language? Which is the real adventure: spending three grand on a mach-one MiG jet ride over Kamchatka, or spending the same sum exploring the cities and villages of Siberia by train and motorcycle? Does getting to know your scuba divemaster in South Africa carry any more personal potential than chatting up a stranger ten minutes from your home? Indeed, what is the *adventure* in traveling such great distances and achieving such daring acts if (like any workaday consumer) you choose your experience in advance and approach it with specific expectations?

The secret of adventure, then, is not to carefully seek it out but to travel in such a way that it finds you. To do this, you first need to overcome the protective habits of home and open yourself up to unpredictability. As you begin to practice this openness, you'll quickly discover adventure in the simple *reality* of a world that defies your expectations. More often than not, you'll discover that "adventure" is a decision after the fact—a way of deciphering an event or an experience that you can't quite explain.

In this way, adventure becomes a part of your daily life on the vagabonding road. "We know from the first step," wrote Tim Cahill, "that travel is often a matter of confronting our fear of the unfamiliar and the unsettling—of the rooster's head in the soup, of the raggedy edge of unfocused dread, of that cliff face that draws us willy-nilly to its lip and forces us to peer into the void." Thus, when you begin your travels, the mere act of riding a third-class train or using a squat toilet might qualify as an adventure. As such novelties become familiar, you can continue to invite the unknown by weaning yourself from your guidebook, avoiding routines, and allowing yourself to get sidetracked. What better recipe for adventure than to put off deciding on your destination until you arrive at a bus station and scan the schedule for unfamiliar names? What better way to discover the unknown than to follow your instincts instead of your plans?

> Rise free from care before the dawn, and seek adventures. Let the moon find thee by other lakes, and the night overtake thee everywhere at home. There are no larger fields than these, no worthier games than may here be played.
>
> —HENRY DAVID THOREAU, *WALDEN*

"Everything that occurs out of necessity, everything expected, repeated day in and day out is mute," wrote Milan Kundera in *The Unbearable Lightness of Being*. "Only chance can speak to us. We read its message much as gypsies read the images made by coffee grounds at the bottom of the cup." By definition, divining chance means leaving yourself open to both good and bad experiences. Good judgment can come from bad experiences; good experiences can come from bad judgment. The key in all of this is to *trust* chance, and to steer it in such a way that you're always learning from it. Dare yourself to do simple things you normally wouldn't consider—whether this means exploring a random canyon, taking up an invitation to dine with a stranger, or just stopping all activity to experience a moment more fully. These are the kinds of humble choices—each of them as bold as bungee jumping—that lead not only to new discoveries but to an uncommon feeling of hard-won *joy*.

As you make these humbly daring choices, you'll find that adventure is very much a personal pursuit. One of my favorite descriptions of adventure came in an e-mail from Tom Bourguignon (an American traveler I originally met in Cairo), who itemized his top Asian travel adventures as follows:

1. Hanging out with a Dutch couple in southern Laos, and one night we had a contest to see which animals we could induce to eat the most moths: a cat, a chicken, a gecko, or a dog.

2. Getting into a shoving match with a burly Pakistani man in a basement bar in Saigon at about 4 A.M., because of a disagreement about billiard rules—then singing Guns N' Roses songs together, arm in arm, a few minutes later.

3. Finding a waterfall buried deep in the jungle in southern Laos and sitting there all day, just listening.

4. Wandering around back alleys in Cairo with a de-mented Hungarian flautist, looking for some mythical

(and probably nonexistent) coffee shop said to serve up strong ganja in their *sheesha* pipes.

5. Climbing Mount Kinabalu on Borneo, the highest mountain in Southeast Asia at 4,100 meters (not a difficult climb, but thrilling anyway).

Not everyone would find adventure in the same quirky, insouciant situations as Tom, but that's the point. Adventure is wherever you allow it to find you—and the first step of any exploration is to discover its potential within yourself. "Explore your own higher latitudes," wrote Thoreau in *Walden*. "Be a Columbus to whole new continents within you, opening new channels, not of trade, but of thought."

As with many great explorers from years past, a good portion of your travel adventures will come about by accident. Some of these accidents will be positive and serendipitous—like the time I got left behind by my train at the Russia-Mongolia border, then enjoyed a singularly madcap trans-Siberian car chase trying to catch up to it. At other times, of course, travel accidents can be downright awful—like the time I wandered into a cholera epidemic in southern Laos, and ended up puking my guts out for three days in a primitive jungle hospital. The trick to being a good adventurer, of course, is to take all such surprises in stride. "Good people keep walking whatever happens," taught the Buddha. "They do not speak vain words and are the same in good fortune and bad."

With this is mind, you should view each new travel

> The man who is truly good and wise will bear with dignity whatever fortune sends, and will always make the best of his circumstances.
>
> **—ARISTOTLE,** *ETHICS*

frustration—sickness, fear, loneliness, boredom, con-flict—as just another curious facet in the vagabonding adventure. Learn to treasure your worst experiences as gripping (if traumatic) new chapters in the epic novel that is your life. "Adventurous men enjoy shipwrecks, mutinies, earthquakes, conflagrations, and all kinds of unpleasant experiences," wrote Bertrand Russell. "They say to themselves, for example, 'So this is what an earth-quake is like,' and it gives them pleasure to have their knowledge of the world increased by this new item."

In maintaining this open attitude toward misadven-ture, of course, it's important that you don't get carried away and inadvertently *seek* misadventure. It's wise, for example, to keep a positive, adventuresome spirit while you endure malaria (as I did once, in a Bangkok hospi-tal), but it's foolish to invite such a misadventure through sloppy health habits. In the same way, getting robbed (as I was once, in Istanbul) might be rationalized afterward as part of the grand drama of travel, but it's stupid to let your theft defenses go soft merely to keep things interesting.

I mention these two things—sickness and crime—because they are the most preventable misadventures on the vagabonding road. You can easily keep your health up, for example, by staying well rested (even if this means traveling at a slower pace than you'd planned), drinking lots of bottled water, and keeping yourself clean (which includes habitually washing your hands before meals). Pretrip immunizations are vital, of course, but disease prevention should also be a part of your day-to-day habits, especially in regard to how you eat. Indeed, daring yourself to eat exotic foods (from boiled sheep's eyes to fried palm grubs to haggis) should be a deliber-ate part of your adventure—but suffering from exotic gastrointestinal sicknesses should not. An old colonial slogan that still makes a useful starting point in dealing with food is "If you can cook it, boil it, or peel it, you can eat it—otherwise, forget it." When eating at restaurants and food stands, look for establishments with lots of customers (always a sure sign of tasty eats) and healthy-looking employees. Make sure that any meat you order is well cooked when you're in less-developed countries—and be wary of milk (which may not be pasteurized), "beef" (which may not be beef), leafy salads (which likely haven't been washed with purified water), and shellfish. Nonpurified water (ice included) should generally be avoided. Also, be sure to check your bottled water for a broken seal (which often means that the bottle has been fished out of the trash and refilled with tap water).

When you first start traveling, don't react to strange foods or unorthodox routines by undereating. Regardless of your food preferences (such as vegetarianism), make sure you maintain a balanced diet, with lots of fruits, vegetables, grains, and protein. If you aren't too daring in the culinary department—or if you think you'll disagree with the food in certain areas—bring along vitamin supplements. Indulge yourself in "Western" food from time to time, but keep in mind that a restaurant's food isn't necessarily healthy (or clean, or tasty) merely

> The pleasure in traveling consists of the obstacles, the fatigue, and even the danger. What charm can anyone find in an excursion when he is always sure of reaching his destination, of having horses ready waiting for him, a soft bed, an excellent supper, and all the eases and comfort he can enjoy in his own home! One of the great misfortunes of modern life is the want of any sudden surprise, and the absence of all adventures. Everything is so well arranged.
>
> —THÉOPHILE GAUTIER,
> *WANDERINGS IN SPAIN*

because the place has an English-language menu and serves up pizza, club sandwiches, or an "American" breakfast. In Pushkar, India, I once ate lunch at a restaurant that "specialized" in Indian, Mexican, Chinese, Italian, Greek, and Israeli food—and I find it no small coincidence that I suffered stomach problems quite soon after.

Of all the gastrointestinal hazards in faraway lands, a tough one to avoid is traveler's diarrhea, which is caused not just by tainted food but by general changes in diet and climate. The best way to deal with "traveler's D" is to simply keep well hydrated and eat bland foods (rice, bread, yogurt) for a few days, until it improves. If any kind of sickness persists for more than a few days, it can't hurt to relate your symptoms to a local doctor or pharmacist. Most will be familiar with local maladies and happy to set you up with inexpensive prescriptions for whatever ails you. (Of course, a small first-aid kit full of bandages, antiseptic, painkillers, and personal medicines should already be a part of your travel gear.) If your sickness threatens to get serious, make your way to a major city and check into a modern hospital.

Crime and scams are common wherever travelers are found, though they are generally no more dangerous than the average annoyances in your hometown. All it takes to avoid such theft is a little awareness. Many local scams are detailed in guidebooks, for example, so be sure to study up whenever you arrive in a new region. (Word of mouth among travelers is also a good way to keep tabs on this.)

Wherever you go, however, a few basic precautions will always apply. For starters, avoid bringing expensive or irreplaceable items on the road, and don't flaunt what wealth you do have. Keep cash and traveler's checks in discreet places (such as a money belt, a sock, or a hidden pocket), and be wary of public distractions and dense crowds, as this is where pickpockets tend to operate. When staying at a hotel or guesthouse, keep your extra cash in the safe (and write out an itemized receipt with the clerk to ensure that everything is in order when it comes time to retrieve your things).

In tourist areas, be wary of pushy new "friends" who insist on giving you free shopping or sightseeing tours. Don't fall into quick-money schemes (with locals *or* travelers) that entail gem or carpet export, duty-free resales, exchange-rate margins, or drugs—these are *all* time-honored scams. Don't wander around drunk at night, and don't let nosy locals know that you've been in their country for only a few days (this marks you as an easy sucker for con artists—better to fudge a bit and claim you've been there for a month). In maintaining this awareness against theft and scams, don't overcompensate and fall into knee-jerk paranoia (a sure way to ruin your experience anywhere); instead, cultivate a simple and instinctive habit of diligence as you travel. I'm writing this book in a peaceful residential hotel in southern Thailand, for instance, but I always padlock the door when I leave my room. I simply find it easier to keep a habit of caution than to continually try to guess when things are and are not safe.

> We have no reason to mistrust our world, for it is not against us. Has it terrors, they are our terrors; has it abysses, those abysses belong to us; are dangers at hand, we must try to love them. . . . How should we be able to forget those ancient myths about dragons that at the last moment turn into princesses; perhaps all the dragons of our lives are princesses who are only waiting to see us once beautiful and brave.
>
> —RAINER MARIA RILKE, *LETTERS TO A YOUNG POET*

Though prevention and diligence go a long way, of course, there is no foolproof method against misadventure on the road. Should sickness or crime catch you off guard, the best response is to humbly accept these things as a part of life's adventure. "Life has no other discipline to impose, if we would but realize it, than to accept life unquestioningly," wrote Henry Miller. "Everything . . . we deny, denigrate or despise, serves to defeat us in the end. What seems nasty, painful, evil, can become a source of beauty, joy and strength, if faced with an open mind. Every moment is golden for him who has the vision to realize it as such."

Once you actualize this vision in good fortune and bad, you'll be able to discover and explore a whole new kind of terra incognita within yourself.

Tip Sheet

ONLINE TRAVEL HEALTH RESOURCES

U.S. Centers for Disease Control and Prevention (http://www.cdc.gov/travel)
Official inoculation and health recommendations for international travelers. Online database includes updated international health news and travel health tips for every country in the world. A great starting point for health and vaccination information about your destination.

Travel Health Online (http://www.tripprep.com)
A well-organized and comprehensive health website for travelers. Gives extensive listings on individual countries, including level of medical care, economic and political

standing, vaccination issues, and possible health concerns.

Lonely Planet Health Check (http://www.lonelyplanet
.com/health)
A well-organized online health guide, including predeparture health planning information, women's health concerns, and specific disease information. Lonely Planet also publishes a Healthy Travel series of small, easy-to-pack health guides, with separate volumes for Africa, Asia, Oceania, and Latin America.

TRAVEL HEALTH BOOKS

Shitting Pretty: How to Stay Clean and Healthy While Traveling, by Jane Wilson-Howarth (Travelers' Tales, 2000)
A humorous, sympathetic approach to travel health, including tips on how to avoid diarrhea, parasites, and all manner of tropical diseases.

Staying Healthy in Asia, Africa, and Latin America, by Dirk Schroeder (Avalon Travel Publishing, 2000)
An easy-to-pack and user-friendly handbook to travel health in developing countries.

The Pocket Doctor: A Passport to Healthy Travel, by Stephen Bezruchka (Mountaineers Books, 1999)
A small, easy-to-pack guide to identifying and avoiding ailments on the road.

Rough Guide to Travel Health, by Nick Jones, Pema Sanders, and Charles Easmon (Rough Guides, 2001)

Includes a section on pretrip health planning, an encyclopedia of health problems, and an international section dedicated to specific countries' health risks.

For a fully updated and linkable online version of this resource guide, surf to http://vagabonding.net/ and follow the "Resources" link.

VAGABONDING VOICES

All foreign travel is an adventure for me. It's about opening the mind and challenging the soul. If that means climbing Everest, knock yourself out. If that means shopping at a souk with two thousand screaming Arabs, that's good too.

—PAUL MCNEIL, 36,
CITY PLANNER, CALIFORNIA

———

Adventure is stretching your boundaries. It is more of a process than a thing, and involves a certain amount of hardship, and is the travel rather than the end. Sometimes that involves going somewhere that most visitors do not go. Sometimes it is a particularly trying day where something good happens at the end. And then there is something about finding magical spots that make all the work worthwhile.

—CHARLES STONE, 25,
STUDENT, CALIFORNIA

Life is adventure. Travel is adventure with a different address. "Seek and you shall find" is not an adage that works in this case. Adventure has a way of finding people, and some people find it more often than others.

—WENDY WRANGHAM, 31,
JOURNALIST, ENGLAND

———

Adventure can be whatever makes you smile—in the short or long term. (You might not be smiling now, but if you survive, you will!) I don't really look for adrenaline rushes, and my best adventures would be totally dull to someone else. It is so often circumstance that makes an adventure, not a place or an action.

—LIESL SCHERNTHANNER, 35,
SEASONAL ANTARCTICA
LABORER, IDAHO

The Pioneering Women of Vagabonding

Travelers are privileged to do the most improper things with perfect propriety. That is one charm of traveling.

—ISABELLA LUCY BIRD,
UNBEATEN TRACKS IN JAPAN

Historically, adventure travel is too often seen as the exclusive pursuit of rugged men, from Richard Burton to Earnest Shackleton to Edmund Hillary. A quick review of travel accounts from the last 250 years, however, reveals that many of history's most intrepid and insightful adventurers were women.

Mary Wollstonecraft, Isabella Lucy Bird, Alexandra David Neel, Mary Kingsley, Freya Stark, Frances Trollope, Amelia Edwards, Emily Hahn, Ida Pfeiffer, Rosita Forbes, Rose Wilder Lane, Rebecca West, and Martha Gellhorn represent a mere sampling of women who won renown for their adventures. They traveled to places as far-flung as Arabia and the Arctic, Africa, and the American frontier.

In addition to shattering the stereotype that brawn and machismo are prerequisites to striking off into the wilderness, these female explorers also found adventure in human encounters and the simple day-to-day unknown. Isabelle Eberhardt, who explored North Africa in the nineteenth century, unapologetically summed up the logic that fired these pioneering women vagabonders: "The cowardly belief that a person must stay in one place is too reminiscent of the unquestioning resignation of animals, beasts of burden stupefied by servitude and yet always willing to accept the slipping on of the harness. There are limits to every domain, and laws to govern every organized power. But the vagrant owns the whole vast earth that ends only at the non-existent horizon, and her empire is an intangible one, for her domination and enjoyment of it are things of the spirit."

PART **IV**

The Long Run

CHAPTER 8

Piety and conformity to them that like,

I am he who tauntingly compels men, women, nations,

Crying, Leap from your seats and contend for your
lives!

Who are you that wanted only to be told what you
knew before?

Who are you that wanted only a book to join you in
your nonsense?

—WALT WHITMAN, "BY BLUE
ONTARIO'S SHORE"

Keep It Real

Though now considered to be one of the great monuments of ancient civilization, the lost city of Angkor was not even known to the Western world until French travelers began exploring Cambodia in the mid–nineteenth century. Contrary to popular belief, the massive, awe-inspiring Khmer ruins were first discovered and documented not by explorer Henri Mouhot but by Charles-Emile Bouillevaux, a French priest who visited the site in 1850.

Having been trained in the strict ways of piety, Bouillevaux was somewhat horrified by the sight of the ancient
stone city, with its voluptuous sculptures and "pagan"
motifs. One year after Bouillevaux published his weak-
kneed observations in Paris, Mouhot stumbled across
Angkor and viewed the ancient city not through the eyes
of his discipline (he was a naturalist) but with naive eyes
of wonder and curiosity. When Mouhot's travel account
was eventually published, the public shared in his exuberance, and Angkor has been a site of archaeological
study and pilgrimage ever since.

In recounting this story, it's tempting to write off Father Bouillevaux as a pious nitwit—but most of us tend
to make the same mistakes when we travel. Just like the
stuffy French priest, we tend to view our new surroundings through the petty prejudices of home rather than
seeing things for what
they are. "Our eyes find
it easier on a given oc-
casion to produce a
picture already often
produced, than to seize
upon the divergence
and novelty of an im-
pression," wrote Fried-
rich Nietzsche. "It is difficult and painful for the ear to
listen to anything new; we hear strange music badly."
Unlike Bouillevaux, most of us don't stand to lose our
place in the history books if we misinterpret the discoveries of our travels. Nevertheless, it's important, even on
a personal level, to not just look at things as we travel
but to *see* things for what they are.

This difference between looking and seeing on the
road is frequently summed up with two somewhat op-
posable terms: *tourist* and *traveler*. According to this dis-

> The use of traveling is to regulate imag-
> ination by reality, and instead of think-
> ing how things may be, to see them as
> they really are.
>
> —SAMUEL JOHNSON, FROM
> *ANECDOTES OF SAMUEL JOHNSON*

tinction, travelers are the ones who truly "see" their surroundings, whereas tourists just superficially "look" at attractions. Tourists, moreover, are thought to lack depth and taste, and their pursuits are considered inauthentic and dehumanized; travelers, interested and engaged, are exactly the opposite. For the past century or so, critics and travel writers have fleshed out this tourist/traveler contrast with an entire canon of aphorisms:

> "The traveler sees what he sees," wrote G. K. Chesterton in the 1920s, "the tourist sees what he has come to see."

> "The traveler was active, he went strenuously in search of people, of adventure, of experience," Daniel Boorstin opined in 1961. "The tourist is passive; he expects interesting things to happen to him."

> "Tourists don't know where they've been," observed Paul Theroux twenty years ago, "travelers don't know where they're going."

> "Travelers are those who leave their assumptions at home, and [tourists are] those who don't," wrote Pico Iyer in 2000.

These are all apt observations, of course, but they have inadvertently contributed to an odd perversion of the very idea they're trying to communicate. Indeed, so well known is the rhetorical difference between tourists (whom we scorn) and travelers (whom we want to be) that the distinction has turned into a social exercise instead of an experiential one. Once, while hanging out in Dahab, Egypt, I talked to a British fellow who had nothing but contempt for what he called "tourists." "They all fly straight to Sharm el-Sheikh [a ritzy resort town near Dahab] and spend their time in luxury hotels," he said. "They might take an air-con bus to see Mount Sinai, but apart from that, they just sunbathe and eat pizza like they could do at home. None of them really experiences Egypt." I agreed that this kind of travel left a lot to be desired, but the more the guy talked, the more I wondered how he considered himself any different. In four months of travel, he'd spent three and a half months living in a reed hut in Dahab—and he'd spent most of his time there scuba diving and smoking dope with other travelers. The only lifestyle difference I could discern between him and the "tourists" of Sharm el-Sheikh was that he ate falafel, wore a black-checkered Arab *kaffiyeh*, and survived on eight dollars a day instead of two hundred.

I mention this not to condemn the guy's lifestyle, but to point out how the tourist/traveler distinction has largely degenerated into a cliquish sort of fashion dichotomy. Instead of seeking the challenges that true travel requires, we can simply point to a few stereotypical "tourists," make some jokes at their expense, and consider ourselves "travelers" by default.

> **Most people are on the world, not in it—having no conscious sympathy or relationship to anything about them— undiffused, separate, and rigidly alone like marbles of polished stone, touching but separate.**
>
> **—JOHN MUIR, *THE WILDERNESS WORLD OF JOHN MUIR***

In reality, travel is not a social contest, and vagabonding has never represented a caste on the tourist/traveler hierarchy. Depending upon circumstance, a sincere vagabonder could variously be called a traveler *or* a tourist, a pilgrim or a satyr, a victor or a victim, an individual seeker or a demographic trend. Indeed, the main conceit in trying to distinguish travelers from tourists is that you end up with a flimsy facade of presumed insiders and outsiders. By the vacuous standards of fashion, insiders and outsiders are necessary, but in the realm of travel (where, by definition, you are always a guest in foreign places) such a distinction is ridiculous. Putting on a cocksure and superior air may win you points at a nightclub in your hometown, but such pretense on the road will only cheapen your travel experience.

Instead of worrying about whether you're a tourist or a traveler, the secret to "seeing" your surroundings on the road is simply to *keep things real*.

On the surface, this seems like a simple enough proposition. "Wherever you go, there you are" says a silly adage—and simply *being there* shouldn't be a very tough task. The thing is, few of us ever "are" where we are: Instead of experiencing the reality of a moment or a day, our minds and souls are elsewhere—obsessing on the past or the future, fretting and fantasizing about other situations. At home, this is one way of dealing with day-to-day doldrums; on the road, it's a sure way to miss out on the very experiences that stand to teach you something.

This is why vagabonding is not to be confused with a mere vacation, where the only goal is escape. With escape in mind, vacationers tend to approach their holiday with a grim resolve, determined to make their experience live up to their expectations; on the vagabonding road, you prepare for the long haul knowing that the predictable and the unpredictable, the pleasant and the unpleasant are not separate but part of the same ongoing reality. You can try to make vagabonding conform to your fantasies, of course, but this strategy has a way of making travel irrelevant. Indeed, vagabonding is—at its best—a *rediscovery* of reality itself.

Thus, as the initial days of your travel experience stretch into weeks and months, you should let go of your pretrip stereotypes and exchange two-dimensional expectations for living people, living places, and living life. This process is the only way to break through the static postcard of fantasy and emerge into the intense beauty of the real. In this way, "seeing" as you travel is somewhat of a spiritual exercise: a process not of seeking interesting surroundings, but of being continually interested in whatever surrounds you.

> For my part, I travel not to go anywhere, but to go. I travel for travel's sake. The great affair is to move; to feel the needs and hitches of our life more nearly; to come down off this feather-bed of civilization, and find the globe granite underfoot and strewn with cutting flints.
>
> —ROBERT LOUIS STEVENSON,
> *TRAVELS WITH A DONKEY*
> *IN THE CÉVENNES*

In many ways, embracing reality is daunting—not because of its hazards but because of its complexities. Thus, the best way to confront reality is not with a set method of interpretation (which will allow you to recognize only patterns you already know) but with a sincere attitude of open-mindedness.

The challenge in cultivating open-mindedness, of course, is that this very notion can get confused before you ever leave home. While traveling the Middle East, for instance, I once met a Canadian woman who'd just traveled to a remote Syrian Catholic monastery in the gorgeous desert mountains outside of Damascus. Not only had she enjoyed her three-day visit, she told me, but she'd also managed to hold on to her "freethinking principles" by steadfastly refusing the monks' offers to join the daily church service. Somehow, this attitude struck me as a bit skewed. In the conformist confines of small-town Alberta, refusing to go to church might be a sign of liberation, but as the guest of an isolated Syrian monastery (one that you've taken great pains to visit, no less), refusing to go to church is not merely narrow-minded but rude. It's important to remember that what passes for cultural open-mindedness at home won't always apply wholesale to your travels. Indeed, you might live in Chinatown, dance to Fela Kuti tunes, wear a sarong, practice the didgeridoo, date an Estonian-American, and eat enchiladas in New York—but that doesn't necessarily mean you know squat about how the people of China, Nigeria, Thailand, Australia, Estonia, or Mexico live and think.

Interestingly, one of the initial impediments to open-mindedness is not ignorance but ideology. This is especially true in America, where (particularly in "progressive" circles) we have politicized open-mindedness to the point that it isn't so open-minded anymore. Indeed, regardless of whether your sympathies lean to the left or the right, you aren't going to learn anything new if you continually use politics as a lens through which to view the world. At home, political convictions are a tool for getting things done within your community; on the road, political convictions are a clumsy set of experiential blinders, compelling you to seek evidence for conclusions you've already drawn.

> Luxury, then, is a way of being ignorant, comfortably.
>
> —LEROI JONES, "POLITICAL POEM"

This is not to say that holding political beliefs is wrong—it's just that politics are naturally reductive, and the world is infinitely complex. Cling too fiercely to your ideologies and you'll miss the subtle realities that politics can't address. You'll also miss the chance to learn from people who don't share your worldview. If a Japanese college student tells you that finding a good husband is more important than feminist independence, she is not contradicting your world so much as giving you an opportunity to see hers. If a Paraguayan barber insists that dictatorship is superior to democracy, you might just learn something by putting yourself in his shoes and hearing him out. In this way, open-mindedness is a process of listening and considering—of muting your compulsion to judge what is right and wrong, good and bad, proper and improper, and having the tolerance and patience to try to see things for what they are.

Another ironic impediment to reality is the very idealism that inspires us to travel in the first place. In our travel daydreams, we transport ourselves to places that we believe will be prettier, purer, and simpler than what we encounter at home. When these idealized conditions prove less than real, however, we tend to cling to our daydreams instead of fully engaging reality. In some cases, such as the "ethno-tourism" villages I discussed in chapter 6, we cheat reality by overlooking the details (blue jeans or cell phones) that don't match up to our premodern ideals. In other cases, the naive optimism we bring into travel causes us to ultimately disdain the very cultures we'd idealized. While I was living in Pusan, for example, I met many expatriate teachers who'd moved overseas to "experience another culture," only to become embittered when they discovered that Korean culture could be downright cutthroat and workaholic. These folks were "experiencing another culture" all right—but their myopic idealism backfired on them when they realized that an Asian society could be just as frenetic and impersonal as their own. In this way, any idealized search for the Other threatens disappointment in a world where the Other can often resemble home.

Just as skepticism should not be confused with cynicism, however, embracing realism need not be confused with falling into pessimism. One particularly potent strain of traveler pessimism is the notion that modern influences are destroying native societies, or that certain cultures were more "real" sometime in the not-too-distant past. According to this assumption, any given society—Kuna or Bedouin or Masai—was somehow better twenty years ago, before it was "spoiled." What such reflexive pessimism overlooks, of course, is that societies have always changed, and that "tradition" is a dynamic phenomenon. "The evaluation of tourism cannot be accomplished against a static background," wrote tourism scholar Davydd J. Greenwood. "Some of what we see as destruction is construction. Some is the result of a lack of any other viable option; and some the result of choices that could be made differently."

Beyond this, much of our concern about the evils of change within premodern cultures is less an interest in the quality of local life than our own desire to experience an "untainted" culture. As anthropologist Claude Lévi-Strauss pointed out fifty years ago, mourning the perceived purity of yesterday will only cause us to miss the true dynamic of today. "While I complain of being able to glimpse no more than the shadow of the past," he wrote in *Tristes Tropiques*, "I may be insensitive to reality as it is taking shape at this very moment. . . . A few hundred years hence, in this same place, another traveler, as despairing as myself,

> The unreal never is: the Real never is not. This truth indeed has been seen by those who can see the true.
>
> —FROM THE *BHAGAVAD GITA*

will mourn the disappearance of what I might have seen, but failed to see."

Thus, the purest way to see a culture is simply to accept and experience it as it is *now*—even if you have to put up with satellite dishes in Kazakhstan, cyber cafés in Malawi, and fast food restaurants in Belize.

After all, as Thomas Merton retorted when asked if he'd seen the "real Asia" during his trip to India, "It's *all* real as far as I can see."

One final reality-numbing process worth mentioning is the pursuit of fun on the road. Fun, of course, can be had in any given moment of your travels—but I'm thinking specifically about that bedrock institution of fun: *partying*. To be sure, your travels won't be the same if you don't occasionally take the time to put on a buzz, let your inhibitions down, and get to know new people. When you first hit the road, in fact, you probably won't be able to party enough, as the company will seem superb, the drinks cheap, and the settings perfect.

As you get past the first few weeks of your travel experience, however, you'll discover that partying on the road is different from partying at home. At home, partying is a way of celebrating the weekend, or taking a pause from the workaday world; on the road, every day is a weekend, every moment a break from the workaday world. Thus, falling into a nightly ritual of partying (as can easily happen at traveler hangouts anywhere on the planet) is a sure way to overlook the subtlety of places, stunt your travel creativity, and trap yourself in the patterns of home. Granted, you can have plenty of fun in the process—but if you travel the world merely to indulge in the same kinds of diversions you enjoy at home, you'll end up selling your vagabonding experience short.

Of all the intoxicants you can find on the road (including a "national beer" for nearly every country in the world), marijuana deserves a particular mention here, primarily because it's so popular with travelers. Much of this popularity is due to the fact that marijuana is a relatively harmless diversion (again, provided you don't get caught with it) that can intensify certain impressions and sensations of travel. The problem with marijuana, however, is that it's the travel equivalent of watching television: It replaces real sensations with artificially enhanced ones. Because it doesn't force you to work for a feeling, it creates passive experiences that are only vaguely connected to the rest of your life. "The drug vision remains a sort of dream that cannot be brought over into daily life," wrote Peter Matthiessen in *The Snow Leopard.* "Old mists may be banished, that is true, but the alien chemical agent forms another mist, maintaining the separation of the 'I' from the true experience of the 'One.'"

Moreover, chemical highs have a way of distracting you from the utterly stoning natural high of travel itself.

> Often I feel I go to some distant region of the world to be reminded of who I really am. . . . Stripped of your ordinary surroundings, your friends, your daily routines, your refrigerator full of your food, your closet full of your clothes, you are forced into direct experience. Such direct experience inevitably makes you aware of who it is that is having the experience. That's not always comfortable, but it is always invigorating.
>
> —MICHAEL CRICHTON, *TRAVELS*

After all, roasting a bowl might spice up a random afternoon in Dayton, Ohio, but is it really all that necessary along the Sumatran shores of Lake Toba, the mountain basins of Nepal, or the desert plateaus of Patagonia?

As Salvador Dalí quipped, "I never took drugs because I *am* drugs." With this in mind, strive to *be* drugs as you travel, to patiently embrace the raw, personal sensation of *unmediated reality*—an experience far more affecting than any intoxicant can promise.

Tip Sheet

All too often, "responsible travel" is a notion that gets hijacked by ecotourism marketers and political demagogues. Fortunately, responsible travel doesn't require that you become an ecotour client or a shrill activist. Rather, conscientious vagabonding merely requires informed awareness as you travel from place to place. And for all the talk about ecological and cultural sustainability, few people actually *understand* these concepts. Knowing your *science*—not your politics—is what will best inform your decisions as you tread lightly through the world.

Basic Ecology, by Ralph Buchsbaum, Mildred Buchsbaum, and Lisa Uttal (Boxwood Press, 1957, reprinted 2002)
Over the years, this classic textbook has enlightened scores of students about the principles of ecology. This reprint edition has new material but retains the basic concepts of earth science, including carbon and nitrogen cycles, food webs, biomes, periodic changes, and ecological succession.

Foundations of Ecology: Classic Papers with Commentaries, edited by James H. Brown and Leslie A. Real

For a more academic and theoretical approach to environmental science, this anthology features forty classic papers that helped lay the foundations of modern ecology.

Native Tours: The Anthropology of Travel and Tourism, by Erve Chambers (Waveland Press, 1999)
A readable academic exploration into the cultural and environmental conséquences of travel.

Hosts and Guests: The Anthropology of Tourism, edited by Valene L. Smith (University of Pennsylvania, 1989 reprint)
First published in 1977, this collection of academic essays takes a look at the complex interrelations between travelers and locals—and how they affect one another.

State of the World, edited by Worldwatch Institute (W. W. Norton & Company, 2002)
An annual report regarding social and environmental sustainability around the globe. Occasionally alarmist, but very well researched. A companion website (http://www .worldwatch.org) features articles and live chats about a variety of global issues, including tourism.

SUSTAINABLE TRAVEL RESOURCES ONLINE

Planeta.com (http://www.planeta.com)
A clearinghouse for practical ecotourism around the globe, with an emphasis on Latin America. Features online forums, conference information, and more than ten thousand pages of features and scholarly reports. The best ecotravel resource online.

Tourism Concern (www.tourismconcern.org.uk)
A U.K.-based nongovernmental organization specializing in ethical, sustainable, and environmentally responsible tourism. Publishes various books about ethical tourism, as well as an informative quarterly magazine, Tourism in Focus.

For a fully updated and linkable online version of this resource guide, surf to http://vagabonding.net/ and follow the "Resources" link.

VAGABONDING
VOICES

Don't travel in order to get away from anyplace. Do it to be wherever you are that night when you go to sleep. And if you are not happy with where you are or what you're doing, it is all right to move on, or just give up and go home.

—EAMONN GEARON, 31,
WRITER, ENGLAND

I have learned that, at the end of the day, we are more or less all the same—there are wonderful and horrible people in every culture and city and pueblo in the world. I have become more realistic because of travel, realizing that people around the world all have the same basic needs and wants.

—DAN NEELY, 26,
RAFT GUIDE, ARIZONA

While trekking in Nepal, I sometimes got tired and cranky and didn't like sleeping in a dirt room adjoining the stable with cattle banging against the wall all night. When living in a thatched bungalow in Yap, I occasionally longed for air-conditioned comfort. I didn't like being pawed by vendors in northern Vietnam; my legs hurt as I crouched for two days on the ancient wooden boat sweeping down the Mekong River in Laos. I keep reminding myself why I'm doing what I'm doing—my goal is to experience another culture as it is, and not look for the easy way out, not try to sanitize the experience. Overall, the discomforts are few and are far outweighed by the joy of discovery.

—LINDA ROSE, 58,
RETIRED TEACHER, OREGON

Travel has taught me a lot about patience (and its cousin tolerance), and self-reliance. To turn the old "New York, New York" song on its head, I've found that if you can make it anywhere, you can make it there (wherever "there" is).

—JOHN BOCSKAY, 30,
TEACHER, NEW YORK

Ed Buryn

The "danger" of vagabonding resides in having your eyes opened—in discovering the world as it really is.
                    —ED BURYN, *VAGABONDING IN EUROPE*
                              AND NORTH AFRICA

In the 1970s, when counterculture excesses threatened to degrade Jack Kerouac's ecstatic road visions into a self-indulgent caricature, Ed Buryn's offbeat travel guides redeemed independent travel for everyday vagabonders. Mixing inspiration with down-to-earth advice, Buryn's *Vagabonding in Europe and North Africa* and *Vagabonding in the U.S.A.* inspired a generation of travelers to disregard the clichés of fashion and seek the simple joy of direct experience on the road.

Raised in New Jersey and Florida by Polish-immigrant parents, Buryn has over the course of his life been a sailor, a professional photographer, a publisher, a writer, an editor, a designer, and a poet.

In *Vagabonding in Europe and North Africa,* Buryn underscored that long-term travel is not the exclusive realm of rebels and mystics but is open to anyone willing to embrace the vivid textures of reality: "We all have stuck in us deep somewhere a keenness for excitement, a savoring for the kooky, a leap-for-life outlook. From this comes the catalytic impetus, without which all other requirements mean nothing. Everyday types are as likely to have this *sine qua non* as the obvious icon-kickers. The person who strikes off for himself is no hero, nor necessarily even unconventional, but to a greater degree than most people, he or she thinks and acts independently. The vagabond frees in himself the latent urge to live closer to the edge of experience."

CHAPTER 9

Travel is a creative act—not simply loafing and inviting your soul, but feeding on the imagination, accounting for each fresh wonder, memorizing, and moving on. . . . And the best landscapes, apparently dense or featureless, hold surprises if they are studied patiently, in the kind of discomfort one can savor afterward.

—PAUL THEROUX, *TO THE ENDS OF THE EARTH*

Be Creative

In countless caper movies over the years, the goal of the protagonists has been to steal an eye-popping sum of money (a million dollars is always a good amount) and escape to some tropical paradise in a quiet corner of the world. To successfully reach this faraway Shangri-la, loot in hand, is what constitutes a happy ending—and not much screen time is devoted to what happens after. The implication here is that a stack of money and a tropical hideaway provide the ideal ingredients for personal happiness, and that nothing better could be asked from life than to sit around and drink rum cocktails until death finally claims you.

As with many things cinematic, of course, this scenario is an escapist cliché, and you don't need to rob a bank to prove it. Indeed, just take a modest, nonheisted sum—five grand, say—to a quiet, inexpensive beach in Guatemala, Greece, or Goa and see what happens. In all likelihood, your enthusiasm for sitting around smeared in·cocoa butter will run out before your money does. This is not because tropical beaches in these places are boring (to the contrary, they are some of the most beautiful and blissful spots in the world) but because what most people consider "paradise" is defined in contrast to the stresses of home. Take away those stresses for a couple of months, and it's hard to wring much passion or esteem from hanging out on a beach and not doing much.

Few vagabonders restrict their travels to one beach scene, of course; but the point is that you can't ever dream up the perfect travel formula while you're still sitting at home. What seems like paradise when you're planning your travels—be it white-sand beaches, archaeological wonders, or exotic textile markets—will eventually seem somewhat normal after a few weeks or months of living on the road. Moreover, so many new things will happen in the process of reaching these places that you'll probably outgrow your original travel motivations. As new experiences and insights take you in surprising new directions, you'll gradually come

> Scope eludes my grasp, there is no finality of vision,
> . . . tomorrow a new walk is a new walk.
>
> —A. R. AMMONS, "CORSONS INLET"

to understand why longtime travelers insist that the journey itself is far more important than any destination.

At times, in fact, the sheer wealth of options in your journey will seem overwhelming. One of the most stressful moments on my first trip across Asia, for example, came not from some physical or emotional trauma but from reading discount-travel ads in the *Bangkok Post*. Every major region in the Eastern Hemisphere, I discovered, was reachable from Thailand for under four hundred dollars. Within two days (and at no great expense) I could have found myself in Paris, Beirut, Melbourne, Tokyo, Cape Town, or Bali and embarked on a completely different and amazing new adventure than the one I was starting in Thailand. When I checked into my Khao San Road guesthouse that night, I could hardly sleep. Had I really made the right choice in coming to Southeast Asia? Hadn't I, after all, always wanted to see Australia? Might Africa have provided a wilder adventure? Didn't Europe promise more romance?.

In retrospect I see that my stress wasn't the product of indecision; the conflict arose from my impossible desire to be in all those places at once. In knowing that so many destinations were cheaply accessible at that very moment, I suddenly feared I would never again get the chance to see them. Travel, I was coming to realize, was a metaphor not only for the countless options life offers but also for the fact that choosing *one* option reduces you to the parameters of that choice. Thus, in knowing my possibilities, I also knew my limitations. Ultimately, I learned to stop looking at my journey as one final, apocalyptic chance to see the world, and started enjoying it on its own, esoteric terms. As I learned to focus my travel energies onto my immediate surroundings, I eventually stretched what I thought might be a one-year Asia sojourn into thirty intense months.

I still haven't been to Australia or much of Africa, I might add—but my explorations in Asia gave me the patience and confidence to know that I *will* see those places in time.

> Powerful men do not necessarily make the most eminent travelers; it is rather those who take the most interest in their work that succeed the best; as a huntsman says, "It is the nose that gives speed to the hound."
>
> —FRANCIS GALTON, *THE ART OF TRAVEL*

In this way, vagabonding is less like a getaway caper than a patient kind of aimlessness—quite similar, in fact, to what the Australian Aborigines call "walkabout." Culturally, the walkabout ritual is when Aborigines leave their work for a time and return to their native lifestyle in the outback. On a broader and more mythical level, however, walkabout acts as a kind of remedy when the duties and obligations of life cause one to lose track of his or her true self. To correct this, one merely leaves behind all possessions (except for survival essentials) and starts walking. What's intriguing about walkabout is that there's no physical goal: It simply continues until one becomes whole again.

In making reference to Aboriginal mysticism, I'm not suggesting that the goal of vagabonding is to become whole. After all, wholeness implies closure, and vagabonding is an ongoing process of finding new things. You can, however, recover and discover *parts* of yourself—psychic and emotional parts you never knew existed—as you travel through the world. And, as you do this, you'll also *leave behind* aspects of yourself—habits, prejudices, even pieces of your heart.

Striking the right balance between finding yourself and losing yourself on the road, of course, requires creativity.

Creativity is particularly important after you've been on the road for a long time, because inevitably you'll fall into a kind of road routine. Certain activities—sleeping, eating, reading, socializing, wandering—will become a fixture of each day. This is good and well (routines make your day more efficient, after all), but you should be careful not to let your days or destinations blur together. Once this begins to happen—once you feel yourself getting jaded to the long haul—it's time to mix your travels up a bit.

How you choose to do this will depend on how you've already been traveling. If you've mainly been visiting cities, for example, perhaps it's time to hit the countryside. If you've been spending most of your time in the backcountry, try a taste of city life. If you've been traveling alone, seek out new companions. If you've been traveling with a partner, split up for a while. If you haven't done much recreation yet, rent a kayak, take an open-water scuba course, or learn how to rock climb. If all you've done is play, maybe it's time to head out and wander with no particular goal in mind.

> Listen: we are here on earth to fart around. Don't let anybody tell you any different!
>
> —KURT VONNEGUT, *TIMEQUAKE*

Sometimes it's not a bad idea to take a break from your shoestring budget and indulge yourself in a gourmet dinner or a night in a luxury hotel, just to see how the other half travels. At other times, buying into a crowded group tour of a local site can be an interesting (and an ironically entertaining) change of pace from independent travel. Occasionally, when you feel like you've overdosed on local color, you might want to catch a taste of home. One of my guilty pleasures of Bombay, for example, was watching the movie *Charlie's Angels* on the big screen after eating a burger at an American-style diner. (The following day I had nearly as much fun watching a four-hour Bollywood musical, and trying to decipher the Hindi plot.)

One surefire method to keep travel from getting too predictable is to occasionally acquire or improvise your own transportation. In Laos, I bought a local fishing boat with some other travelers and drove it down the Mekong River for three adrenaline-filled weeks. In Burma, I bought a Chinese-made one-speed bicycle in Mandalay and pedaled it south for ten days before trading it for a fistful of pearls. In Lithuania, I stuck out my thumb on the side of the road in Vilnius, and found myself four countries away (in Hungary) three days later. In Israel, I did away with transport altogether and walked across Galilee, Jesus-style. In addition to being unforgettable experiences, each of these adventures ended up costing me next to nothing. I still intend to try other classic forms of self-transport, such as a used car in Australia, a used horse in Argentina, a used camel in Morocco, and an off-the-assembly-line Enfield motorcycle in India.

However (or wherever) you happen to travel, your experience of a place will obviously be different if you stay there for two days, two months, or two years. Most places you'll only be able to experience for a few days, of course, but just because you're traveling doesn't mean you must always be on the move. "What dost thou think then of seeing the world?" taunts Peleg in Herman Melville's *Moby-Dick*. "Can't ye see the world where you stand?" With this in mind, it's advisable to pick an appealing place at some point in your travels and settle down for a few weeks or months to get to know it better.

Where you choose to do this is entirely up to your whim. Perhaps you'll linger at a place you'd always dreamed of knowing; perhaps you'll happen upon a place (or a person) that you fall in love with; or maybe you'll just go on instinct. In two and a half years of traveling the Orient, I lingered for three weeks or more in Bangkok, Riga, Cairo, and Pushkar. My reasons for hanging out in each location were not always that inspired (in Pushkar, for example, I was trying to get some rest and overcome a bout of stomach sickness); rather, each experience just sort of *made sense* as I was living it. "While wandering, you experience a mysteriously organic process," observed Joseph Campbell. "It's like a tree growing. It doesn't know where it's growing next. A branch may grow this way and then another way. When you look back, you'll see that this will have been an organic development." Thus, you'll often find that your decision to linger someplace is a simple flowering of your ongoing explorations.

> People say you have to travel to see the world. Sometimes I think that if you just stay in one place and keep your eyes open, you're going to see just about all that you can handle.
>
> —PAUL AUSTER, *SMOKE*

Once you've found a special place to call your own for a few weeks or months, your options there are virtually endless—and you needn't have a concise plan going in. "There are deeper reasons to travel—itches and tickles on the underbelly of the unconscious mind," wrote Jeff Greenwald in *Shopping for Buddhas*. "We go where we need to go, and then try to figure out what we're doing there." At the outset, you might linger in a place just to slow down, goof off, and rest up for more travel. Should you want to catch up on some reading, feel free to string up a hammock and plow your way through a stack of books. Should you have hobbies—cooking, painting, music, meditation—you might take this time to deepen and diversify such interests within an exotic new context.

Should you feel more social, you might choose to wander through your adopted hometown and figure out the inner workings of the place: how the houses are made, how the food is cooked, how the crops are farmed (at times you might even be invited to lend a hand in these activities). In the process, you can make local friends by joining in lighthearted public activities, such as soccer matches, backgammon games, or afternoon cocktails. You might even learn unexpected things about local customs, religions, or values merely by observing the habitual rhythms of the day. Should aimless curiosity not fit your disposition, however, there are plenty of more structured ways to experience a destination. Many places, for example, will offer classes in local disciplines (Thai massage, Italian cooking, Indian yoga, Argentine tango), and language classes anywhere are a great way to immerse yourself in a local culture.

Work is another way to deepen your experience of places as you travel. Rarely will you find travel jobs that make you lots of money, but you should at least be able to break even on living expenses while meeting interesting people and finding unique experiences. Teaching English is a popular (and easy-to-find) work option on the road, but there are plenty of alternatives—many of them dealing with the labor or hospitality industries. Farmwork, for example, is a common traveler's employment in New Zealand. Fruit

> If you really want to learn about a country, work there.
>
> —CHARLES KURALT, *A LIFE ON THE ROAD*

harvest is a seasonal job option in France. Labor in kibbutz collectives (usually farms or factories) is a time-honored traveler's option in Israel. Landing a job at a hostel or a resort is often an opportunity in areas of the world with heavy tourist traffic. None of these jobs are all that glamorous, of course, but they allow you to make a bit of cash while you view certain corners of the world from a new angle. The evenings I spent working as a bar tout in Jerusalem didn't earn me much travel money, for example—but all those hours of handing flyers to disinterested pedestrians allowed me to learn humility in a way that enriched my perspective of the city. Though such work need not be arranged before you start your travels, specialty publications such as *Transitions Abroad* magazine (see the resource tip sheet at the end of this chapter) are great for finding out what short-term jobs and volunteer opportunities are out there.

Should making money not be a factor, volunteer work is another great, inexpensive way to get to know a place. When I traveled across North America, for instance, none of Mississippi's tourist attractions were as memorable as the days I spent hauling concrete for a volunteer house-building project outside of Canton. Such volunteer pursuits can be directed toward randomly discovered situations as you travel (for example, briefly lending your medical, carpentry, or English skills as you come across communities in need). Other volunteer work—from building irrigation systems in El Salvador to teaching computer skills in Tibet—can be found through more formal routes, such as state agencies, religious groups, and nongovernmental aid organizations. However you choose to donate your skills, try to be honest with yourself and do so out of a personal calling instead of some vague sense of obligation or patchwork political morality. Volunteer work, after all, is serious business, and you stand to harm more than help the cause if your convictions are less than true.

Be patient in finding your volunteer work, and be humble in *doing* your volunteer work. In most cases, volunteers to a certain area end up learning as many lessons as they teach. This is why volunteering is not just socially but *personally* useful, since it will leaven your idealism with eye-opening doses of reality. "Learning about fundamental, and at times unbridgeable cultural and historical gaps between peoples is essential," noted travel writer and ex–Peace Corps worker Jeffrey Tayler. "One must not delude oneself that we are all alike or destined to be members of some sort of global family." Indeed, acknowledging differences and avoiding superficial cures is not just a valuable lesson of volunteer work—it's often the *first step* in actually solving the problems that you seek to fix.

> We travel, initially, to lose ourselves; and we travel, next, to find ourselves. We travel to open our hearts and eyes and learn more about the world than our newspapers will accommodate. We travel to bring what little we can, in our ignorance and knowledge, to those parts of the globe whose riches are differently dispersed. And we travel, in essence, to become young fools again—to slow time down and get taken in, and fall in love once more.
>
> —PICO IYER, "WHY WE TRAVEL"

However you choose to enrich your experience of a place—be it through building a recreation center, harvesting grapes, or playing pickup games of chess at the local café—always challenge yourself to try new things and keep learning.

In this way, you'll find that you're not just exploring new places but weaving a tapestry of life experience that is much richer and more intricate than you could ever have imagined while you were still at home.

PUBLICATIONS: OVERSEAS WORK AND
VOLUNTEERING

***Transitions Abroad* magazine** (http://www.transitions
abroad.com)
*A bimonthly magazine detailing affordable alternatives to
mass tourism. A fantastic practical resource for anyone
looking to mix overseas work and travel for months and
years at a stretch; $28 for a one-year (six issues) sub-
scription. The companion website makes a great portal
for researching travel and volunteer opportunities. Transitions Abroad also publishes the annual* Alternative Travel
Directory, *which outlines current travel, study, and living
opportunities worldwide.*

***The Back Door Guide to Short-Term Job Adventures: In-
ternships, Extraordinary Experiences, Seasonal Jobs, Volunteering, Work Abroad,*** by Michael Landes (Ten Speed
Press, 2001)
*Insider tips and resources for finding short-term work and
volunteer opportunities overseas.*

Work Your Way Around the World, by Susan Griffith (Vaca-
tion-Work, 2001)
*Advice on how to find short-term work around the world.
Much of the resource information is geared more toward
British (rather than North American) travelers.*

How to Live Your Dream of Volunteering Overseas, by
Joseph Collins, Stefano Dezerega, Zahara Heckscher, and
Anna Lappe (Penguin USA, 2002)
Useful resource information on volunteering in Latin

America, Africa, Asia, eastern Europe, and the Middle East. Includes case studies, worksheets, and quotes from international volunteers.

Volunteer Vacations: Short-Term Adventures That Will Benefit You and Others, by Bill McMillon and Edward Asner (Chicago Review Press, 1998)
A listing of more than 250 charitable organizations and 2,000 projects worldwide that are looking for volunteers.

VOLUNTEER AGENCIES

Peace Corps (http://www.peacecorps.gov)
Sending Americans off on worldwide volunteer projects since 1961. "The toughest job you'll ever love."

Institute for International Cooperation and Development (www.iicd-volunteer.org)
Trains and sends volunteers abroad for development and aid work in Africa and Latin America.

Volunteers for Peace (http://www.vfp.org)
This Vermont-based organization offers inexpensive short-term voluntary service programs in more than eighty countries.

WWOOF: Willing Workers on Organic Farms (http://www .wwoof.org)
This exchange organization gives you room and board in return for your help in working and managing an organic farm or smallholding. Membership is inexpensive, and programs are available worldwide.

OVERSEAS WORK AND VOLUNTEERING
RESOURCES ONLINE

The Frontier Club (http://www.work4travel.co.uk)
An online resource for short-term work opportunities around the world, including cruise-ship work, bartending, kibbutz labor, fruit harvesting, and carpentry.

Idealist.org (http://www.idealist.org)
An online database for overseas jobs and volunteer opportunities worldwide.

International Volunteer Programs Association (www.volunteerinternational.org)
An up-to-date search site for international volunteer opportunities.

EscapeArtist.com (http://www.escapeartist.com)
An online portal for information on how to live, work, and invest overseas.

iAgora.com: Work and Study Abroad Solutions (http://www.iagora.com)
An online community for overseas work, study, and travel. Emphasis on Europe.

For a fully updated and linkable online version of this resource guide, surf to http://vagabonding.net/ and follow the "Resources" link.

VAGABONDING
VOICES

I think traveling really opens your eyes to the reality that anything, from a very easy life (a sort of permanent island-vacation life), to a totally wild and wacky life, is completely attainable. In my travels I meet countless people with different experiences—people who have lived on a beach in Bali or Thailand or Greece for several years or who have taught in Turkey or South America, etc. The more you travel, the more travelers you meet, which means more and more options are constantly presented to you. As a result, my mind is always entertaining a hundred different possibilities, and I feel less and less responsibility or obligation to return to the 'daily grind' of a regular, normal job and lifestyle back in America.

—LAVINIA SPALDING, 32,
TEACHER, ARIZONA

I've always felt that for me to truly understand and grow I would have to live and work in a place for a long period of time. I still believe this is true but have found that I can stay in a place for a few months, study the language, and really work at meeting local people and still accomplish the same task.

—BARBARA AKEY-LEONARD, 33,
TEACHER, ARIZONA

———

Traveling can be as varied as one wants it to be. There are mountains and villages and beaches and so much to learn and experience and see. If you think that your travels are becoming monotonous because you are road weary, find a place you enjoy and stay for a while to regain your strength. If that doesn't work, pack it up, come home, and get back into the "rut." After fighting traffic to go and sit in a cubical somewhere five days a week, week after week, you will know monotony. I would bet that you would be planning your next trip in no time.

—SHIRLEY BADOR, 46,
TRAVEL AGENT, GEORGIA

The Vagabonders of Pax Islamica

I have indeed—praise be to God—attained my desire in this world, which was to travel through the earth.

—IBN BATTUTA

Though it may be tempting to view vagabonding purely as a pastime of the industrialized West, long-term travel was for centuries a primarily Eastern art. Indeed, some of the most vivid personal accounts of vagabonding come from the tenth through the fifteenth centuries, when safe travel was possible within an Islamic empire that stretched from the pillars of Hercules on the Atlantic to the Malayan archipelago of Southeast Asia.

While Ibn Battuta is the most celebrated of these Arab travelers (see chapter 6), men like Ibn Jubayr of Spain and al-Muqaddasi of Jerusalem also wandered to the far corners of the Islamic world, gaining life experience along the way (and earning their keep) as teachers, lawyers, hawkers, bookbinders, papermakers, merchants, messengers, and pilgrims. Not all of these vagabonders were Muslim, either: One of the most prolific travelers in the time of Pax Islamica was Benjamin of Tudela, a Spanish rabbi whose twelfth-century adventures took him as far as the western border of China.

In *The Meadows of Gold*, tenth-century Muslim geographer al-Masudi described the thirst for diverse experience that inspired the wanderers of this era: "He who stays at home beside his hearth and is content with the information which he may acquire concerning his own region, cannot be on the same level as one who divides his life span between different lands, and spends his days journeying in search of precious and original knowledge."

CHAPTER 10

People say that what we are all seeking is a meaning for life. I don't think this is what we're really seeking. I think what we're seeking is an experience of being alive.

—JOSEPH CAMPBELL, *THE POWER OF MYTH*

Let Your Spirit Grow

There's another story that comes from the ancient Desert Fathers of Egypt. In this tale, a monk named John the Dwarf decided one day that life in the monastery was too much work and didn't quite match up to his spiritual ideals. "I should like to be free of all care," he confessed to his abbot, "like the angels who do not work, but ceaselessly commune with God." Taking his cloak and a bit of food, John the Dwarf then went away into the desert.

About a week later, in the middle of the night, the abbot heard a faint knock on the door of the monastery. "Who is it?" the abbot demanded. "It is I, your brother John the Dwarf," came the meek reply. "You must be confused," the abbot retorted wryly, leaving the door bolted. "For John the Dwarf has become an angel, and no longer lives among men." The following morning, the abbot unlocked the monastery to find a distressed John the Dwarf huddled on the stoop. "Ah, it appears that you are a man after all," the clever abbot said, "and that you must once again work in order to live."

In seeking to find epiphany in some ill-conceived departure from reality, John the Dwarf was not the first person in history to make a spiritual fool of himself—and he certainly wasn't the last. Indeed, the modern travel scene in general has a notorious reputation for such half-baked spiritual foolery, as many wanderers tend to confuse simple exoticism with mystical revelation. The guru-of-the-month seekers in India and the "Jerusalem syndrome" crackpots of the Holy Land are just a couple of vivid stereotypes in a long tradition of self-indulgent travel "mysticism."

Fortunately, embracing the spiritual side of travel doesn't require that you don a robe and lose your mind. What we know as personal travel, after all, is the historical legacy not of exploration or commerce but of *pilgrimage*—the nonpolitical, nonmaterial quest for private discovery and growth. Indeed, regardless of whether or not you consider your vagabonding journey to be "spiritual," self-motivated travel has always been intertwined with the personal workings of the soul.

But on an even simpler level, heightened spiritual awareness is the natural result of your choice to put the material world in its place and hit the road for an extended time. Where your treasure is, your heart will be also—and your decision to enrich your life with time and experience (instead of more "things") will invariably pay spiritual dividends. Travel, after all, is a form of asceticism, which (to quote Kathleen Norris) "is a way of surrendering to reduced circumstances in a manner that enhances the whole person. It is a radical way of knowing exactly who, what, and where you are, in defiance of those powerful forces in society that aim to make us forget."

> The world is wilder in all directions, more dangerous and bitter, more extravagant and bright. We are making hay when we should be making whoopee; we are raising tomatoes when we should be raising Cain and Lazarus.
>
> —ANNIE DILLARD, *PILGRIM AT TINKER CREEK*

Thus, travel compels you to discover your spiritual side by simple elimination: Without all the rituals, routines, and possessions that give your life meaning at home, you're forced to look for meaning within yourself. And just as John the Dwarf had to "work in order to live," this spiritual process is not always free of care. Indeed, if travel is a process that helps you "find yourself," it's because it leaves you with nothing to hide behind— it yanks you out from the realm of rehearsed responses and dull comforts, and forces you into the present. Here, in the fleeting moment, you are left to improvise, to come to terms with your raw, true Self.

As prosaic and practical as this process sounds, it is actually in keeping with time-honored spiritual traditions. Jesus, after all, taught that it's pointless to look to otherworldly realms for revelation, because "the kingdom of God is within you." The Buddha expressed enlightenment not as a mystical firestorm but as the disassembling of the conditioned personality. The Ecclesiastes of the Hebrew tradition asserts that "a live dog is better off than a dead lion," because God favors what you do *now*. Islam asserts that the sacred is never separate from the secular, and that the world itself has spiritual lessons to teach.

In learning the spiritual lessons of travel, of course, you may discover that it's not always possible to share or express what you are experiencing. Religious traditions have given us certain words and metaphors to describe the numinous realm—but words are symbols, and symbols never resonate the same for everyone. Many people, for instance, saw Jack Kerouac's *On the Road* as a secular celebration of speed and freedom, but to Kerouac, the book was a spiritual diary. "It was really a story about two Catholic buddies roaming the country in search of God," he wrote in a 1961 letter to Carroll Brown. "And we found him. I found him in the sky, in Market Street San Francisco, and Dean had God sweating out of his forehead the whole way." Traditional Catholics might question Kerouac's characterization of the divine, of course, but the discrepancy is more a matter of semantics than inspiration.

> It is not speech which we should want to know: we should want to know the speaker.
> It is not things seen which we should want to know: we should know the seer.
> It is not sounds which we should want to know: we should know the hearer.
> It is not the mind which we should want to know: WE SHOULD KNOW THE THINKER.
>
> —FROM THE KAUSHITAKI UPANISHAD

Often, spirituality is best approached without specific lexicons or set formulas. Too frequently on the road, people seek the spiritual side of life in the same determined way they might join a gym: They want results, and they want them soon. Thus, the yoga camps of

India, the meditation retreats of Thailand, and the evangelical group tours of Galilee sell out (literally and figuratively) to vacationers in search of instant spiritual gratification. In reality, there is just as much epiphany to be had in wandering lost through the alleyways of Varanasi, enduring diarrhea on the Bangkok–to–Surat Thani minibus, or playing games with children in the Nazareth town square. Moreover, spirituality is an ongoing process that deepens with the seasons—and those who travel the world hoping to get "blinded by the light" are often blind to the light that's all around them.

At a certain level, then, spiritual expression requires the same kind of openness and realism that is required of vagabonding in general, particularly in culturally reversed situations (which can be found not only in distant Lhasa or Rishikesh but in the Near Eastern confines of Jerusalem or Mount Athos). "There is no God but Reality," goes a saying attributed to a mythical Sufi sect—and, blasphemous as this sounds, it is not a declaration of unbelief. Rather, it is a warning to avoid turning inspiration into fetish and tradition into dogma; it is an admonition to never reduce the spiritual realm to the narrow borders of your own perceptions, prejudices, and ideals.

> We must assume our existence as broadly as we in any way can. Everything, even the unheard-of, must be possible in it. That is at bottom the only courage that is demanded of us: to have courage for the most strange, the most singular and the most inexplicable that we may encounter.
>
> —RAINER MARIA RILKE, *LETTERS TO A YOUNG POET*

Indeed, if you travel long enough, you'll find that your spiritual revelations are invariably grounded in the everyday. A great little vignette of spiritual discovery comes from Joshua Geisler, an American musician I met in India. Though Josh originally traveled to India for its musical and mystical tradition, his very idealism was what initially kept him from growing as a musician. During his first few lessons with an Indian flute master, he would inquire only about the mystical side of the music. But, as Josh told me in an e-mail, the experienced teacher invariably steered the lesson back to the functional challenges of his art:

> *"But what about Tansen," I would ask, "is it really true that he could light a fire with his voice?"*
>
> *With a chuckle, the master would answer: "Why sing a* raga, *when you could just light a match?"*

Eventually, Josh came to realize that the flute master's very practicality—his faith in technical diligence—was what enhanced his capacity for true spiritual expression while playing music.

Ultimately, then, discovering the sacred as you travel is not an abstract quest so much as a manner of perceiving—an honest awareness that neither requires blind faith nor embraces blind doubt.

And, more often than not, the most singular experiences of travel come in *not finding* what you'd hoped to discover. In *The Snow Leopard* (thought by many to be the best travel book of the last century), there is ironic joy in the fact that Peter Matthiessen *never sees* a snow leopard during his adventure in the Himalayas. Thus, robbed of a climactic moment, Matthiessen leads us into the simple essence of his journey: "the common miracles—the murmur of my friends at evening, the clayfires of smudgy juniper, the coarse, dull food, the hardship and simplicity, the contentment of doing one thing at a time: when I take my blue tin cup into my hand, that is all I do."

Whoever you are! motion and
    reflection are especially for you,
The divine ship sails the divine sea for
    you.
Whoever you are! you are he or she for
    whom the earth is solid or liquid,
You are he or she for whom the sun
    and moon hang in the sky,
For none more than you are the
    present and the past,
For none more than you is
    immortality.

—WALT WHITMAN, "A SONG OF THE
ROLLING EARTH"

Before you begin your travels, you might not see the spiritual significance of such seemingly mundane details. After all, a journey is a temporary diversion, and there would seem to be little reward in the "common miracles" it promises.

That is, until you realize that life itself is a kind of journey.

Tip Sheet

An eloquent meditation on life, death, and nature, set in the Virginia wilderness.

The Road Within: True Stories of Life on the Road, edited by Sean O'Reilly, James O'Reilly, and Tim O'Reilly (Travelers' Tales, 1997)
A collection of spiritual travel writing from authors like Annie Dillard, Barry Lopez, and Natalie Goldberg.

Art of Pilgrimage: The Seeker's Guide to Making Travel Sacred, by Phil Cousineau (Conari Press, 1998)
A well-written guide to finding spiritual resonance in everyday travel.

The Way of the Traveler: Making Every Trip a Journey of Self-Discovery, by Joseph Dispenza (Avalon Travel Publishing, 1999)
A book about using travel for spiritual growth and deeper life experience.

One Thousand Roads to Mecca: Ten Centuries of Travelers Writing About the Muslim Pilgrimage, edited by Michael Wolfe (Grove Press, 1999)
An anthology of writings about the biggest spiritual travel event in the world—the Muslim pilgrimage to Mecca—as seen through the eyes and hearts of the people who've made the hajj over the last thousand years.

SACRED TEXTS: A SAMPLER

The Bible: Ecclesiastes
The most concise, powerful, and universally relevant book of wisdom in the Jewish tradition.

The Bible: The Gospel of Matthew, the Gospel of Luke
Two engrossing accounts of the life and teachings of Jesus, as told by Matthew (a Jewish tax collector) and Luke (a Greek physician).

The Dhammapada, translated by Eknath Easwaran (Nilgiri Press, 1986)
An accessible translation of the sutra that is as essential to the Buddhist tradition as the Sermon on the Mount is to the Christian tradition.

The Essential Koran, translated by Thomas Cleary (Book Sales, 1998)
A collection of readings from the Koran, designed to help non-Muslim Westerners appreciate the power and poetry of the Muslim holy book.

Tao Te Ching: A New English Version, translated by Stephen Mitchell (Harper Perennial, 1992)
A Zen-influenced translation of Lao Tzu's classic meditations.

The Upanishads, translated by Juan Mascaro (Viking Press, 1965)
Simple and powerful verses from the ancient mystical tradition of Hinduism.

For a fully updated and linkable online version of this resource guide, surf to http://vagabonding.net/ and follow the "Resources" link.

VAGABONDING
VOICES

Travel, education, spirituality, and social evolution are to me intrinsically intertwined. If we spent half the money on travel that we do on material goods in America I think the world would be a much different place. We've stifled our curiosity because it's time-consuming (and time is money). Travel is spiritual because it's about personal growth, awareness, and sensitivity.

—MISHELLE SHEPARD, 33,
WRITER AND EDITOR,
MISSOURI

———

The most rewarding aspect of long-term travel is discovering what your own core values are. You find out what you believe In and what drives you. Long-term travel is a challenge, but it's the best time you'll ever have if you're ready for it.

—JASON GASPERO, 31,
NEWSLETTER EDITOR,
HAWAII

I find travel to be the best metaphor for spiritual life . . . and I prefer to live it literally. I've been convicted over the years about giving back something to the people in the countries where I travel and take so much from them in terms of knowledge and experience. After guessing roughly at my budget for a particular trip, I set aside ten percent, a "travel tithe," if you will. During that trip, I give away the money if I meet individuals or families with specific needs, and sometimes to religious groups or organizations that I feel are worthy. As a Christian, I believe I'm just a "pilgrim and traveler on this earth" anyway.

—ADAM LEE, 32,
TEACHER, MINNESOTA

Annie Dillard

Beauty and grace are performed whether or not we sense them. The least we can do is try to be there.

—ANNIE DILLARD,
PILGRIM AT TINKER CREEK

Aself-described "wanderer with a background in theology and a penchant for quirky facts," Annie Dillard examines the realm of the spirit through the lens of nature.

Born Annie Doak in 1945 in Pittsburgh, Dillard had a Salingeresque childhood—studying her own urine under a microscope and reading *On the Road* with the encouragement of her father (who himself once quit a job to travel down the Mississippi River). After suffering a near-fatal attack of pneumonia at age twenty-five, Dillard decided that she needed to experience life more fully—so she spent four seasons living alone in the Virginia backwoods. The book she wrote about the experience, *Pilgrim at Tinker Creek* (which blends Christian spirituality with eccentric observations about the natural world) went on to win the Pulitzer Prize.

In her writing, Dillard points out that curiosity about the world is the starting point for spiritual discovery, and vice versa: "What we know, at least for starters, is: here we—so incontrovertibly— are. This is our life, these are our lighted seasons, and then we die. In the meantime, in between time, we can see. The scales are fallen from our eyes, the cataracts are cut away, and we can work at making sense of the color-patches we see in an effort to discover where we so incontrovertibly are. It's common sense: when you move in, you try to learn the neighborhood."

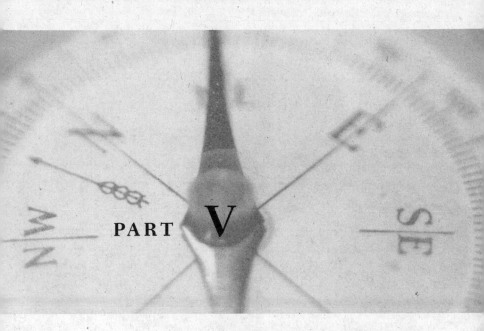

PART **V**

Coming Home

Round the world! There is much in that sound to inspire proud feelings; but whereto does all that circumnavigation conduct? Only through numberless perils to the very point whence we started, where those that we left behind secure were all the time before us.

—HERMAN MELVILLE, *MOBY-DICK*

Live the Story

Of all the adventures and challenges that wait on the vagabonding road, the most difficult can be the act of coming home.

On a certain level, coming home will be a drag because it signals the end of all the fun, freedom, and serendipity that you enjoyed on the road. But on a less tangible level, returning home after a vivid experience overseas can be just plain *weird* and unsettling. Every aspect of home will look more or less like it did when you left, but it will *feel* completely different.

In trying to make sense of this homecoming experience, people often quote T. S. Eliot's "Little Gidding":

> *And the end of all our exploring*
> *Will be to arrive where we started*
> *And know the place for the first time.*

As inspiring as this sounds, however, "knowing" your home for the first time means that you'll feel like a stranger in a place that should feel familiar.

Initially you'll enjoy rediscovering all the little aspects of home that you missed in faraway lands: long, hot showers; the latest movies in full Dolby sound; dinner and drinks at your favorite restaurants and hangouts. But after a few days of indulgence, you'll begin to feel a strange sensation of homesickness . . . for the road.

Your old friends will offer absolutely no help in this regard. As exciting and life-changing as your travel experiences were, your friends will rarely be able to relate, because they don't share the values that took you out on the road in the first place. You may have shared your soul with a fellow traveler you'd known for two hours in Zambia, but for some reason you'll be unable to get your closest friends to break out of their standard conversation patterns and take an interest in your adventures.

A vivid illustration of this social disparity comes from American vagabonder Jason Gaspero, who wrote me in an e-mail: "One of the most difficult things I experienced in my travels was trying to relate what I'd experienced to old friends and acquaintances who'd been at home the whole time I was gone. When I recounted how I got into a fight with a Javanese transvestite, swam with barracuda, or ate spicy dog with rice, they'd get a glazed look in their eyes. When I finished telling them these stories, there was little response. 'Wow,' they'd say with weak enthusiasm. Then they'd tell me about what happened at the local pub and how they'd hooked up with Sally from college again. Here I'd thought I was missing out on so much when I was gone, but these reunions made me realize I was a changed person."

Encounters such as this will make you realize why travel should always be a personally motivated undertaking. Try as you might, you simply can't make the social rewards of travel match up to the private discoveries. In sharing your road experiences, then, remember to keep your stories short and save the best bits for yourself. "I swear I see what is better than to tell the best," wrote Walt Whitman. "It is always to leave the best untold."

Moreover, telling the story is not nearly as important as *living* the story. Indeed, your vagabonding experience need not be some quaint sand castle that washes away when you return home. If travel truly is in the journey and not the destination, if travel really is an attitude of awareness and openness to new things, then *any moment* can be considered travel. "Objects which are usually the motives of our travels are often overlooked and neglected if they lie under our eyes," wrote Pliny the Younger nearly two thousand years ago. With this in mind, it's important to remember that your vagabonding attitude is not something you can turn on and off when it's convenient. Rather, it's an ongoing, organic process that can be applied even as you unpack your bags and readjust to home. After all, hitting the road to get travel out of your system rarely works, so the best remedy upon returning home is to make travel a *part* of your system.

One immediate reward of such an attitude will be how it instantly connects your home with the rest of the planet. Your travels, you will discover, have awakened you to parts of the world, and awakened parts of the world within you. Experiences and observations that didn't quite make sense on the road will suddenly come into perspective as you once again become a part of your home community. International news about the regions you visited will resonate in a personal way—and you'll come to realize how the mass media can only offer a partial perspective on other places and cultures. As you continue to read, learn, and think about the places you once visited, you'll realize that your travels never fully end. Even in times of solitude at home, you'll feel less like an isolated individual than part of a greater community of people and places, near and far, past and future.

As for the practical challenges of "reentry" into your home life (moving in, finding a job, starting a routine), confront them all as new adventures. Rediscover your work, and do it well. Redeploy your simplicity, and make it pay out in free time. Emulate the best of people who themselves were at home when you met them on your travels. Pinpoint what you learned from them—hospitality, fun, reverence, integrity—and incorporate these things into your own life. Integrate the deliberate pace and fresh perspective that made your travel experience so vivid, and allow for unstructured time in your day-to-day home schedule. Don't let the vices you conquered on the road—fear, selfishness, vanity, prejudice, envy— creep back into your daily life. Explore your hometown as if it were a foreign land, and take an interest in your neighbors as if they were exotic tribesmen. Keep things real, and keep on learning. Be creative, and get into adventures. Earn your freedom all over again and don't set limits. Keep things simple, and let your spirit grow.

But most of all, keep living your life in such a way that allows your dreams room to breathe.

Because you never know when you'll feel the urge to hit the road again.

Allons! The road is before us!

It is safe—I have tried it—my own feet have tried it well—be not detain'd!

Let the paper remain on the desk unwritten, and the book on the shelf unopen'd!

Let the tools remain in the workshop! Let the money remain unearn'd!

Let the school stand! Mind not the cry of the teacher!

Let the preacher preach in his pulpit! Let the lawyer plead in the court, and the judge expound the law.

Comerado, I give you my hand!

I give you my love more precious than money,

I give you myself before preaching or law;

Will you give me yourself? Will you come travel with me?

Shall we stick by each other as long as we live?

—WALT WHITMAN, "SONG OF THE OPEN ROAD"

Acknowledgments

This book was initiated by Joni Rendon (with a big assist from Bill Jenkins), who discovered its rudimentary incarnation on my website, and never faltered in her enthusiasm as the project bloomed. For advice, assistance, and inspiration, past and present, Sarah Jane Freymann, Lynda Ireland, Jeff Lebow, Jen Leo, Cathrine Wessel, and Katie Zug were all a great help in their various ways. Mike Marlett deserves a sentence of his own for his ace Internet assistance. As does Don George, who gave me a golden chance to prove myself at *Salon*. Much love to Alice Potts for her patience, and to big sis Kristin Van Tassel for teaching me how to read, proofing my work over the years, and laughing at every joke I've ever told. And, finally, a heartfelt thanks to everyone I've encountered in my travels—travelers and hosts alike—for your generosity, companionship, and exuberance. Vagabonding wouldn't have been the same without you.

About the Author

Rolf Potts funded his earliest vagabonding exploits by working as a landscaper and an ESL teacher. He now writes about independent travel for *National Geographic Adventure*, and he has been called "the Jack Kerouac of the Internet Age" for his award-winning travel dispatches in Salon.com. His travel essays have appeared in *Condé Nast Traveler*, *National Geographic Traveler*, *Best American Travel Writing 2000*, and on National Public Radio.